Reading Group Choices

Selections for Lively
Book Discussions

Paz & Associates

1996

For further information, contact:

Reading Group Choices
2106 Twentieth Avenue South
Nashville, TN 37212-4312

Phone: (800) 260-8605
Fax: (615) 298-9864
E-mail: DPaz@nashville.net

ISBN 0-9644876-1-6

Cover design by:
Mary Mazer
Art That Works
1651 Grove Street
San Diego, CA 92102
(619) 702-6041

Printed by:
Rich Printing Company, Inc.
7131 Centennial Bl.
Nashville, TN 37209
(615) 350-7300

*A portion of the proceeds from this publication
will be used to support literacy efforts
throughout the United States.*

This publication is dedicated to the authors, agents, publishers, book distributors, and booksellers who bring us books that enrich our lives.

Acknowledgments

This second edition of *Reading Group Choices* was inspired by the many readers who called, wrote and faxed us words of encouragement and appreciation for our first edition in 1995.

We wish to thank participating publishers for their support. This publication was made possible by their financial assistance, and their acknowledgment of the importance of reading discussion groups. Our thanks to: Ageless Press; Banks Channel Books; Beacon Press; Charles River Press; Crown Publishing (division of Random House); Farragut Publishing; Jeremy P. Tarcher (division of Putnam); Jewish Lights Publishing; Knopf (division of Random House); Knowledge, Ideas & Trends; Little, Brown & Company; Longstreet Press; MacMurray & Beck; Papier-Mache Press; Picador USA; G. P. Putnam's Sons; Riverhead (division of Putnam); Spinsters Ink; Sta-Kris, Inc.; Tor Books; Twayne/Macmillan; University of Georgia Press; Vintage Books (division of Random House); Wildcat Canyon Press; and Yes International.

A special thanks to our Advisory Board of readers, reading discussion group leaders, and booksellers who shared their expertise and love of books to screen recommendations: Stephanie K. Freudenthal, *Davis-Kidd Booksellers*, Nashville, Tennessee; Judith S. Gacek, *Village Book & Stationery*, Omaha, Nebraska; Rachel W. Jacobsohn, *Association of Book Group Readers & Leaders*, Highland Park, Illinois; Glenda Martin, *Minnesota Women's Press, Inc.*, St. Paul, Minnesota; Derrick M. Norman, *D & D Enterprises*, Nashville, Tennessee; Janet Rosen, *Women's National Book Association*, New York, New York; and Lynn Page Whittaker, *Charles River Press*, Alexandria, Virginia.

To our readers, who developed discussion topics, we thank Megan DuBois, Barbara Richards Haugen, Kishana Hooks, Trish Labosky, Pat Lane, and Derrick Norman.

For providing their technical expertise and affordable services, we thank Mary Mazer of Art That Works for her cover design, and John Craig and Tom Hutchins of Rich Printing Company, quality book printers since 1892.

And to Mark Kaufman, for sharing his many skills to bring all of the pieces together.

Introduction

Books change lives.

Flip through the pages of this year's edition and you'll discover what an awesome power the written word can have on our lives. Within the pages of the 38 books profiled in this edition, you'll discover information and stories about life, love, family, friendship, politics, our country's poor, clashing cultures, the rapid advancement of technology, creativity, healing, reading, and more.

As in last year's premiere edition, we have developed a collection of titles to offer you diversity – in subject matter, and in works from well-known publishers to new presses. We are happy to introduce a brand new publisher, *Charles River Press,* and their first book *Until We Meet Again: A True Story of Love and Survival in the Holocaust* by Michael Korenblit and Kathleen Janger — a sad, yet inspirational story of love, loss, and faith.

We take special note of two books sure to strike a chord with all life-long readers – *Ruined by Reading: A Life in Books* by Lynne Sharon Schwartz (Beacon Press) and *The Girl Sleuth* by Bobbie Ann Mason (University of Georgia Press). Both will stir memories of reading as a child and of significant books read, and will prompt us to reflect on what reading has meant to us over the years.

The single book we unequivocally recommend to everyone is *Amazing Grace: The Lives of Children and the Conscience of a Nation* by Jonathan Kozol (Crown). You'll be both touched by the insights of the children and angered by our collective disregard for their unimaginable living conditions. Certainly, America can do better.

Through the written word, we can expand our understanding of ourselves and the world around us. We encourage you to support efforts to protect our First Amendment rights and to support literacy efforts so more lives can be improved and enriched through books.

— Donna Paz
Nashville, Tennessee
January, 1996

Contents

Contents (continued)

Contents (continued)

Amazing Grace
*The Lives of Children and the
Conscience of a Nation*

Author:
Jonathan Kozol

Publisher: Crown

First printing: 1995

Available in:
Hardcover, 320 pages, $23.00
(ISBN 0-517-79999-5)

Summary

Amazing Grace tells the stories of a handful of children who have—through the love and support of their families and dedicated community leaders—not yet lost their battle with the perils of life in America's most hopeless, helpless and dangerous neighborhoods. These are children who dream and play and hope, and who remain radiant with grace and possibility thanks to their own courage, and to the efforts of someone who cares. This book begs questions that have no easy answers. Will it matter to such children, who have so little, if they are given even less? Can America afford to save these children—and can it afford to lose them? And what is the ultimate price, on both sides of the poverty line, of turning away from them?

Recommended by Toni Morrison

"Amazing Grace is good in the old-fashioned sense: beautiful and morally worthy."

Author Biography

Jonathan Kozol has spent much of his life talking with and listening to children. His first book, *Death at an Early Age,* won the National Book Award. His book about homeless families, *Rachel and Her Children,* won the Robert F. Kennedy Book Award. His most recent book, *Savage Inequities,* was a finalist for the National Book Critics Circle Award and became a *New York Times* best-seller. Mr. Kozol lives near Boston, Massachusetts.

Topics to Consider

1 Several of the women that Kozol interviews recall a more peaceful and certainly more beautiful Bronx (of the 1940s). Why has the situation in the South Bronx gotten so much worse? If you believe, as Kozol, that no clear cut solutions exist, where does society have to start in order to effect change?

2 Kozol states that "the Ghetto is an evil and unnatural construction" (p.162). Do you agree? Is there anything that can be seen as hopeful and good in these neighborhoods?

3 How do people maintain their faith in the face of such adverse conditions? What does faith do for them?

4 Kozol seems to feel that the nation has regressed since the death of Martin Luther King; he further believes that Dr. King's dream died with him. Why do you feel that this may (or may not) be the case? Might our nation have progressed along different lines had King not been assassinated?

5 Are drugs the overwhelming cause for the marked decline in the South Bronx or an effect?

6 Does the "generation of false optimism" (p. 192) ultimately kill hope?

7 Discuss the concept of "compassion fatigue".

8 Kozol outlines behavior that seems somewhat racist: grocers only making deliveries south of 96th Street, tour books discussing leisure time activities south of 96th Street (pp. 186-187). Do you see this line of demarcation as rational or racist? Explain.

9 Is there any innocence in society's attitudes and behavior toward the South Bronx? Are the efforts being made there misguided? Misunderstood? Is society simply mistaken in its approach? Or do you believe that society is well aware of the impact of its decisions and feels that these neighborhoods should be segregated and maintained as they are currently?

Amazon Story Bones

Author:
Ellen Frye

Publisher: Spinsters Ink

First printing: 1994

Available in:
Quality Paper, 208 pages. $10.95
(ISBN 1-883523-00-1)
Hardcover, 208 pages. $21.95
(ISBN 1-883523-01-X)

Summary

"Once upon a time Amazons lived on the Black Sea coast....
Imagine then a mountain cave in Thrace, 35 years after Troy's last
ember has grown cold. Two old women, an Amazon and a Trojan
slave, fuel the hearthfire with their stories."

Amazon Story Bones is a collection of familiar Greek myths,
retold from a feminist perspective: Melanippe and Marpessa,
Amazon survivors of the Trojan War, instruct and empower Iphito,
a young woman escaping from an arranged marriage, by telling their
story and all the timeless Amazon stories.

Recommended by Elynor Vine, *Visibilities*

*"This is a wonderful, beautifully written book in which every woman will
see not only an aspect of her own quest towards self-awareness, but the
quest of all women everywhere."*

Author Biography

Ellen Frye's connection to Greece began when she lived there in
the early 1960s. Her collection of Greek folk songs, *The Marble
Threshing Floor*, was published in the American Folklore Society
Memoir Series by the University of Texas Press (1972). She is also the
author of the novel, *The Other Sappho* (Firebrand Books, 1989). Ms.
Frye lives in Vermont.

Topics to Consider

1   Marpessa has three intense friendships in her lifetime, with Cassandra, Melanippe, and Thalas. How do these friendships differ from one another and how are they alike?

2   Examining Thetis and her children, the lineage of Melanippe, Marpessa and her daughter and grand-daughter, discuss the relationships between mothers and daughters in these stories.

3   How do these reconstructed Greek myths differ from traditional Greek mythology? Give specific examples.

4   In traditional Greek mythology, the Amazons are savage man-haters conquered by the Greeks — either by Theseus or in the Trojan War. In *Amazon Story Bones*, how are the Amazons portrayed? What are the reasons given here for the conquest of the Amazons by the Greeks?

5   Iphito asks what makes an Amazon and decides that she herself is an Amazon. What might be her destiny as an Amazon? What will she have to overcome or endure, possibly for the rest of her life?

6   Why are images of Amazons so negative? Why do you think it was necessary for Ellen Frye to create a positive image of female goddesses and of the Amazons?

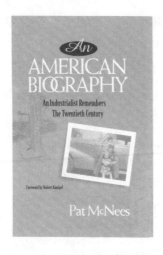

An American Biography
An Industrialist Remembers the Twentieth Century

Author:
Pat McNees

Publisher: Farragut Publishing

First printing: 1995

Available in:
Hardcover, 341 pages. $19.95
(ISBN 0-918535-20-4)

Summary

This engaging narrative of family life in the twentieth century is also the compelling story of an ordinary factory worker who took advantage of extraordinary times to become co-owner of an Ohio manufacturing firm. Warren Webster brings the same gruff but bemused equanimity to company crises, the birth of twins, his wife Mary's crippling bouts of depression (which they weather together through nearly 70 years of marriage), and the joys and perils of old age. By putting a human face on corporate life and an honest face on domestic life, **Pat McNees** has created a story that, as one critic put it, will appeal to "anyone interested in the business of life, the life of a business, and life in these United States."

Recommended by Robin Marantz Henig

"...A story that will resonate for any reader."

Author Biography

An editor and journalist based in suburban Washington, D.C., **Pat McNees** is convinced that the lives of ordinary Americans are as dramatic a subject for biography as the lives of politicians and celebrities, and more valuable as social history. The lingering death of her father led to McNees's next book, the anthology *Dying: A Book of Comfort* (1996).

Topics to Consider

1   Did Warren Webster succeed despite his mother's advice about cautious behavior, or was his mother a role model for his independence? Did Webster steer his own course or did life happen to him?

2   "The best years were the early years," said Webster, when asked which decades of his life were the happiest. Would most people looking back on their lives feel this way or did Webster have a particular reason to do so?

3   Webster's wife Mary was an energetic woman who began experiencing manic depression at the age of 35. Given the times, could Warren and his family have dealt with Mary's illness better than they did? How might it be different for them today? Why do you think Mary's four children reacted so differently from each other to her behavior?

4   What role does Webster's "constancy, reliability, and reason" play in the dramas that unfold around him?

5   Was Warren Webster's balance of work and home life typical for a man? Was he more effective in one arena than in another?

6   Chapter 14 describes a strike that almost destroys Webster's company. Did you find yourself taking sides in this conflict? If so, which side did you choose, and why?

7   Would Webster's company have survived as it did if only one person had been in charge, or was it the interplay of the three owners that made the company work? How would these entrepreneurs fare in today's business climate?

8   Would a Warren Webster starting out today — in an age of conglomerates — have the same chance of success?

9   Mary favors some grandchildren over others and cheats at Yahtzee, a board game she insists they play with her. Yet they adore her. Do we love relatives like Mary despite their worst qualities or because of them? Why do children experience grandparents so differently from parents?

The Artist's Way

A Spiritual Path to Higher Creativity

Author:
Julia Cameron

Publisher: Jeremy P. Tarcher/Putnam

First printing: 1992

Available in:
Quality Paper, 238 pages. $13.95
(ISBN 0-87477-694-5)
Deluxe Gift Edition Hardcover, $24.95
(ISBN 0-87477-831-2)

Summary

The Artist's Way is an empowering book for aspiring and working artists. With the basic principle that creative expression is the natural direction of life, the author leads you through a comprehensive twelve-week program to recover your creativity from a variety of blocks, replacing them with artistic confidence and productivity. Creativity is linked to spirituality by showing in non-denominational terms how to tap into the higher power that connects human creativity with the creative energies of the universe; you are guided through a variety of highly effective exercises and activities that spur imagination and capture new ideas.

Recommended by Martin Scorsese

"This is a book that addresses a delicate and complex subject. For those who will use it, it is a valuable tool to get in touch with their own creativity."

Author Biography

Julia Cameron is an award-winning writer who has been leading creativity workshops for 15 years. She has extensive credits in film, TV, theater, and journalism. She has written for such diverse publications as the *Washington Post* and *Rolling Stone*, and is a published poet who teaches creative writing on the graduate level. She co-authored *The Money Drunk* with Mark Bryan. Ms. Cameron lives in Taos, New Mexico.

Topics to Consider

1 How do you see creativity as a spiritual process?

2 If one isn't religious, would it hinder the ability to be creative?

3 What are the essential challenges that block creativity? What are your personal challenges?

4 What are Morning Pages, and what are the benefits of practicing this technique?

5 What is the Artist's Date, and how can this method be helpful?

6 Why do artists procrastinate and what is procrastination really about? Are you a procrastinator in any way? Share some reasons behind your own procrastination.

7 Discuss the ways you find most effective for overcoming self-doubts. Would these ways be any different for an artist?

8 Describe the qualities of a shadow artist.

9 In what ways can you expand your ability to derive new ideas?

10 In what areas of your life and work would you expect to benefit most from developing your creative self? If you were to use the techniques described by the author over a twelve week period, what might you expect to gain?

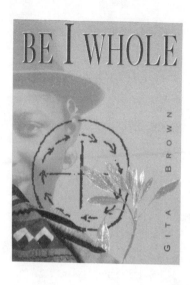

Be I Whole

Author:
Gita Brown

Publisher: MacMurray & Beck

First printing: 1995

Available in:
Hardcover, 267 pages. $16.95
(ISBN 1-878448-66-8))

Summary

A magically real and unflinchingly modern drama about love and family, *Be I Whole* is the choicest of wisdom from a rising voice in American literature. According to Gloria Naylor, author of *Women of Brewster Place*, "[Gita Brown] has a unique vision to add to American literature." *Be I Whole* is the lyrical tale of an ancient and spiritual people struggling to maintain their values in modern America; it forms a rich new parable for our time.

Recommended by *Library Journal*

"On rare occasions, a treasure like this book shines distinctly among the other debut novels of the year...the distinctive characters promise to remain with readers long after the novel has been read."

Author Biography

Gita Brown walks and works between cultures. Her father was a West Indian and a Moslem; her mother is a descendant of the Creek Tribe. A native of Detroit, she is a graduate of the University of Michigan and has an M.F.A. in fiction writing from Brown University. She lives in Providence, RI. In her own words: "I am a storyteller like my ancestors before me. When I write, I often talk out loud to hear the story rather than to see if the words look fine on the page. I want my stories to speak beneath the ink and pulp. What I want is for the listener to hear more clearly what we are all a part of."

Topics to Consider

1   On the first and last pages of *Be I Whole*, the narrator proclaims that this is not a tale but a parable. What does she mean by this?

2   Everything Sizway does and says can be viewed positively or negatively in light of what have in recent years been seen as feminist issues. Though the book is set several decades ago, how is our reading of her actions and her beliefs affected by the current view of women's roles? How do we evaluate the particular matriarchal culture portrayed in the book?

3   What effect does opening the story in downtown Detroit and then moving it to rural Ohio have on the reader? Is it necessary to locate modern questions of family into a pastoral setting to make them clear? If not, then why does the setting change?

4   The author does not seem to be consistent in her use of dialect. How is she able to provide her characters with such strong and recognizable voices without being perfectly faithful to their dialect?

5   The author has said that she wrote the book aloud, revising and rewriting each passage until it *sounded* right. How does that affect the reading experience? And how does it affect our awareness that this novel is being told to us by a pipe-smoking storyteller?

6   Though the effect of *Be I Whole* is that of a traditional, realistic novel, it is marked by a number of events that appear to be magical. What does the author gain by adding an extra level to reality?

7   At what points in the book does the Ki culture intersect with the more mainstream American culture that surrounds it? What does each of those encounters tell us about the Ki? What does it tell us about the dominant culture in Sizway's America? *If* we can attribute the novel's social assertions to the author — that is, if we can assume they are *her* assertions and not just the storyteller's — how do you think she views what has come to be called "multiculturalism"?

The Bird Artist

Author:
Howard Norman

Publisher: Picador USA

First printing: 1994

Available in:
Quality Paper, 320 pages. $13.00
(ISBN 0-312-13027-9)

Summary

This spare, lovely, haunting novel begins in 1911. Its narrator, Fabian Vas, is a bird artist: he draws and paints the birds of Witless Bay, his remote Newfoundland coastal village home. In the first paragraph of his tale Fabian reveals that he has murdered the village lighthouse keeper, Botho August. Later, he confesses who and what drove him to his crime — a measured, profoundly engrossing story of passion, betrayal, guilt, and redemption between men and women — all compressed within the isolated village of the human heart.

Recommended by Anne Whitehouse, *Boston Globe*

"Completely original and compelling...written with great intelligence, wit and clarity."

Author Biography

After graduating from Western Michigan University, **Howard Norman** moved to Canada to work as a writer and researcher, with a special interest in the country's indigenous Indian tribes. In 1977, he first encountered the eastern seaboard of Newfoundland, and learned of the events that led to the story of *The Bird Artist*. He is the author of two previous books, *The Northern Lights*, a 1987 National Book Award finalist, and a collection, *Kiss in the Hotel Joseph Conrad and Other Stories*. His books have been translated into twelve languages.

Topics to Consider

1 Toward the end of *The Bird Artist*, Fabian paints a mural on the church wall. How is Fabian's narration of his story similar to the mural he paints?

2 What role does the theme of isolation, both geographic and emotional, play in Norman's novel?

3 Howard Norman has said that he originally wrote *The Bird Artist* because of Margaret Handle — that "she puppeteers many things in the book." He also "tried to develop landscape as a character." What do Margaret and the landscape of Witless Bay have in common, and how do they shape and affect the book's events?

4 What role do letters, and mail, play in the book? Which characters write letters, and which do not? What purpose does writing play in this narrative?

5 Some critics found mythic qualities in *The Bird Artist*. If a myth is "a traditional story of ostensibly historical events that serves to unfold part of the world view of a people or explain a practice, belief, or natural phenomenon," what does Fabian's story explain or unfold? How does it pertain to the world beyond Witless Bay?

6 How does the community play a role in Fabian's crime and punishment? Although we never "meet" the characters Fabian recalls at his trial, what is their significance?

7 Which view — the comfort of the familiar lighthouse or the opportunity of the vast ocean — does the book, as a whole, support?

8 Norman's protagonists, at various points in the book, commit murder and adultery, lie and steal. Does *The Bird Artist* condone, or even admire, such behavior? What stance does the novel take on religion and the church? Is there religious imagery in Fabian's mural? In the text as a whole?

9 The narrator, Fabian Vas, introduces himself immediately as a bird artist. What is the role of the artist in the book? How does it relate to Fabian's position as narrator, or storyteller?

Computer Tales of Fact & Fantasy

or How We Learned to Stop Worrying and Love the Computer

Editor:
Iris Forrest

Publisher: Ageless Press

First printing: 1993

Available in:
Quality Paper, 160 pages. $9.95
(ISBN 0-9635177-0-8)

Summary

In this anthology you'll find 25 tales by 18 authors. You'll likely identify with most of them. Included are pieces that reflect our current computer world covering ideas that can be enjoyed by past, present and future computer users, as well as those who will never even be tempted to try one. There are true stories, funny ones, fictional ones and a bit of history. There is even some science fiction for sci-fi fans and two short plays for theater lovers.

Recommended by Rob Errera, *Today*

"Whatever your feelings on the current computer age, there's someone represented in this collection that shares your view."

Editor Biography

Iris Forrest's background is in music, theatre, law, ballroom dancing, photography and writing. She started Ageless Press as a creative outlet for writers who wrote about what they knew and loved — their problems and joys with computers.

The biographies of the 18 authors can be found on the pages before each of their stories. They're a diverse group in terms of gender, age and background. Some are professional word pushers, others are actors, musicians, painters, teachers, Realtors, insurance brokers and other business types.

Topics to Consider

1 What effect have computers had on you and your world so far? Are you happy with their influence? What are their plusses and minuses?

2 How have computers changed the business world and ways of conducting business, e.g. working from home instead of an office?

3 Have computers had any effect on the gender gap? Have they penetrated the "glass ceiling"? Have they made it easier or harder for men and women at home? At work?

4 What do you see for the future of computers as they affect education? How might this experience be different for children in poorer schools? And for their future? How will our libraries change with the arrival of the Internet and the World Wide Web?

5 How will computers affect politics, medicine, entertainment, and other arts, including writing?

6 How can we overcome our fear of the unknown and personally benefit from this new technology?

7 Is age a barrier to entering the computer world? Why? Why not?

8 Will printed books become obsolete? Can you see yourself reading a book on a computer screen or printing it out on your own printer for future perusal? If so, what kinds of books are best suited to this application?

9 Does a humorous approach to a serious topic enhance your learning? Which stories did you find most interesting?

10 Can you envision an on-line reading group? Did you know that some already exist? Would you find it easier or more difficult to share personal feelings via this medium? Explain.

Culture Clash

Second Edition

Author:
Ellyn Bache

Publisher: Banks Channel Books

First printing: 1st edition, 1982
2nd edition, 1990

Available in:
Quality Paper, 131 pages. $11.95
(ISBN 0-9635967-0-5))

Summary

When **Ellyn Bache**'s family sponsored a Vietnamese refugee family after the fall of Saigon in 1975, she started a journal to describe the undertaking. She never imagined she'd end up chronicling not just "an" experience but "the" experience American sponsors have with refugees from throughout the world, even more than 20 years later. To the refugees, the U.S. looks immeasurably wealthy — and the sponsors do, too. So when refugees find they're expected to become self-supporting and independent, many feel betrayed. In turn, sponsors are shocked and angry when the refugees expect them to be long-term benefactors. This fascinating account shows how Bache's family developed a way to work through these problems to a nourishing, enriching relationship.

Recommended by N. Gail Magee

"...The book reads like a novel with just enough humor, tragedy and joy to make reading it pleasurable rather than academic."

Author Biography

Ellyn Bache is the author of the novels *Festival in the Fire Season* and *Safe Passage* (which was made into a film starring Susan Sarandon and Sam Shepard), and of the short story collection, *The Value of Kindness*, which won the Willa Cather Fiction Prize. She lives in North Carolina with her family.

Topics to Consider

1   The author realizes that the refugees have fled their country without clothing or survival items, but only with snapshots of their families and tapes of Vietnamese music. The Bache family came up with some theories to explain the refugees' choices and actions. Do you agree with the family's conclusions? If you were forced to flee your home, what would you consider taking?

2   When an article in the local newspaper announces that Kim and Quang need household goods, the author discovers "the many moods of American charity." What does she mean by this? In what ways does her charity — or yours — have "many moods"?

3   When the refugees realize their standard of living is going to drop when they move into their own place, they are obviously dismayed. Yet the sponsors want them to live within their means, as a way of learning to function in the new country. Ultimately, this "tough love" approach works, but at first it makes life difficult for everyone concerned. How would you approach this issue if you were a sponsor?

4   At one point, the author encourages Kim to volunteer at a preschool so she'll be hearing English and getting experience she can use on a resume. But Kim seems to feel she is being exploited. What other expectations might an American family have of Kim and Quang that would make them uncomfortable?

5   Many sponsorships broke down within the first year, because of the same conflicts the Bache family had with Kim and Quang. Are there ways the misunderstandings could have been prevented or at least made less traumatic to each side? How would you set up such a program so that the transition would be easier?

6   The Baches were just one family, with three small children. Many sponsors were churches with large congregations. Each type of sponsorship has its strengths and weaknesses. Is one better than the other? Why?

7   Much of this journal deals with the conflicts that arise when two cultures meet. But in the end, each family was able to admire the other. What features of the Vietnamese culture were attractive to the author? What appeals to you?

8   One commentator wrote, "I dare anyone who reads this book to say America doesn't have a culture!" What do you think she means? Did the book give you insights you didn't have before?

The Divine Mosaic

*Women's Images of
the Sacred Other*

Editor:
Theresa King

Publisher: Yes International

First printing: 1994

Available in:
Quality Paper, 272 pages. $15.95
(ISBN 0-936663-10-3)

Summary

In this rich collection of essays, 24 women from many different spiritual traditions look into the face of God and tell us what they see. Their images of the Sacred Other in prose and poetry form a mosaic that challenges old assumptions and brings the divine fully into the lives of women today.

Recommended by Jean Houston

"The Divine Mosaic is a potent telling of the once and future pieces emerging to fill in the feminine face of God. We are witness here to a mystery as women scholars and seekers from many traditions tell of their deepest encounter with the Divine Feminine. Their words are fire and flame into one's mind. Their images cut to the heart and one knows that the world will never be the same."

Editor Biography

Theresa King is a writer, publisher, and teacher of spirituality. Her work is the expression of a lifetime of study, practice, and worldwide travel. She has spent 22 years with a Himalayan yoga master, seven as his assistant. She holds a B.S. in Education, and M.A. in Human Development and Spirituality. Theresa currently lives in Saint Paul, Minnesota.

Topics to Consider

1 How do you understand the image of a divine mosaic as explained in the editor's preface? Is it an apt metaphor?

2 Did you identify with any one of the essays in particular? Which one? Describe how it speaks to your experience.

3 What are the images you have of divinity? What, in your own religious traditions and culture, have formed these images?

4 Where in your spiritual life do you feel a need for greater nourishment?

5 What is your understanding of and reaction to religious miracles?

6 The writers of the essays in *The Divine Mosaic* come from many different religious traditions. As they describe their experience of the divine, do you see similarities? Differences? Which are more overriding?

7 Many of the authors describe questioning what they had been taught of God. What questions, if any, arose in your mind about what you had been taught?

8 The women in these essays describe their relationship with God. Describe your relationship with God and how it has changed or been influenced by these readings.

9 Discuss Rabbi Weinberg's thought: "The image of the divine may be found when we face someone very different from ourselves and agree to share our wounds and our hopes."

10 Why is the image of God so important in our lives? What does Theresa King mean when she says, "Our God image makes us *do* things ... and *think* things?"

Early Promise, Late Reward

A Biography of
Helen Hooven Santmyer, Author of
"...And Ladies of the Club"

Author:
Joyce Crosby Quay

Publisher: Knowledge, Ideas & Trends

First printing: 1995

Available in:
Quality Paper, 130 pages. $14.95
(ISBN 1-879198-15-0)

Summary

A small town girl from the Midwest, Helen was educated at Wellesley College during World War I and was active in the women's suffrage movement. She sought a publishing career in New York City in the 1920s when most women pursued marriage and family life. She attended Oxford University in England as one of the first female Rhodes Scholars. Returning to the United States with her first book published and a new graduate degree in literature, she felt she was on the verge of long-sought fame and fortune, only to be met by the onset of the Great Depression. It wasn't until she was eighty-eight years old that the media blitz descended on Xenia, Ohio and the world learned of "the old lady who wrote a book."

Recommended by Arthur Schlesinger, Jr.

"Helen Hooven Santmyer was a fine writer and an uncommon woman, and at last with the help of Joyce C. Quay, we can learn about her life of frustration and fulfillment."

Author Biography

Joyce Quay was born in Ohio but grew up and was educated in New York and Boston. She worked in the personnel field while she raised three children and wrote articles when she could, eventually specializing in Ohio people, places and events. *Early Promise, Late Reward* is her first book. She is now working on a history of Mother Goose and enjoying her grandchildren.

Topics to Consider

1   What were the important points in the biography and in Helen's books that illustrate the influence that family and tradition played in her life? Why did she write about them? Was her father too demanding of her, or was she spoiled?

2   Cite examples of Helen having become easily discouraged, and the reasons she might have felt as she did. How would you react, faced with similar circumstances?

3   What influence did Ridgley Torrence have on Helen's life? How might Helen's family have reacted to her interest in a married man?

4   With her education and accomplishments, why did Helen accept life at a small college in a small town for so many years?

5   When Helen's parents died, why did she move back to Xenia? Would that have been the time to try a new life somewhere else?

6   Should Helen Santmeyer be included in American literature and Women's Issues courses in colleges? Why? In what way does Helen speak to young women today?

7   Only *Farewell Summer* was published after Helen's death. How much of Helen's life is revealed in her other four books?

8   How much of an escape did writing *"... And Ladies of the Club"* provide for Helen during her years in Cedarville? Why didn't she try to publish the book years earlier? To what do you attribute its great success?

The Final Judgment

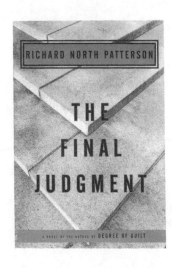

Author:
Richard North Patterson

Publisher: Knopf

First printing: 1995

Available in:
Hardcover, 400 pages. $25.00
(ISBN 0-679-42989-1)

Summary

Caroline Masters has just received a nomination to the Court of Appeals — and a summons to come home, a town where she has not been for more than 20 years, not since she cut herself off from her family after their betrayal of her trust. Now, her niece (whom she has never known) has been charged with murder, and Caroline's father expects her to forget the past to save the family's future. The grip of the past is unshakable, as Caroline finds herself face-to-face with the memories she's kept at bay. She struggles to maintain the "withdrawal of feeling in exchange for thought" that has been the cornerstone of her success. Because not only does the evidence begin to point to an outcome almost as shocking as the crime, but, as her memories return, Caroline finds herself questioning everything about her life.

Recommended by the *San Francisco Chronicle*

"[Caroline]...is that rarest of things in a thriller written by a man: a woman who comes across as a real person with complexity..."

Author Biography

Richard North Patterson has written seven novels, including the international best-sellers *Degree of Guilt* and *Eyes of a Child*. His first novel, *The Lasko Tangent*, won an Edgar Allen Poe Award in 1979. *The Final Judgment* is being developed as a miniseries by NBC. A trial lawyer and law firm partner, he and his wife, Laurie, live with their family in San Francisco and on Martha's Vineyard.

Topics to Consider

1   What motivates Channing Masters? Why is his desire for control so encompassing? He seems to believe that "children do not always live to please their parents, or parents to please themselves". In what ways does he have trouble accepting this philosophy?

2   The reader is often given clues about what lies ahead. This only serves to underscore the fact that before life's most significant events we are caught unaware and unprepared with "no sense of the moment". Do the characters in this book have any sense of recognition that something major is about to occur? How are they disappointed? What is the correlation, if any, between an inability to identify impending events and feeling like a failure?

3   What effect does Nicole Masters' status as a Holocaust survivor have? Discuss the phenomenon of "survivor remorse". How does this influence the choices she makes? Does she pass on a legacy of self-destructive behavior? Is this cycle broken? By whom?

4   Do you believe that the skid marks indicate that Nicole intended to commit suicide and then experienced a change of heart? Or do you believe that she was simply disoriented and realized her error too late?

5   Two summers — in 1964 and in 1972 — mark crucial turning points for a number of characters in *The Final Judgment*. What are these turning points and how do they affect present events?

6   How is Betty similar to her father? How does she seek to control the events and people in her life?

7   How does Caroline's personal involvement with the murder case make it more difficult for her?

8   Was Megan's objective to ruin Brett's life or was she motivated by her own demons?

9   What is the final judgment?

Flying in Place

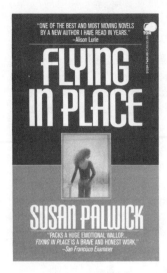

Author:
Susan Palwick

Publisher:
Tor Books

First printing: 1992

Available in:
Mass Market Paperback,
211 pages. $4.99
(ISBN 0-812-51334-7)

Summary

Emma's father is a surgeon, a busy and well-respected figure in the community. Her mother lives a life of the mind, teaching English, reading poetry, keeping alive the memory of Ginny, the perfect sister who died before Emma was born. A perfectly normal family. But every few nights, in the hours just before dawn, Emma's perfectly normal father comes to visit her in her room. In those terrible morning hours, Emma has learned to walk away from her body...on the ceiling, across the room, *anywhere* to be away from the visits...from the breathing. Then on the ceiling one morning, Emma meets Ginny: charming as life, doing cartwheels, flying in place. Ginny knows things Emma doesn't — but it's up to Emma to put the pieces together.

Recommended by Jane Yolen

"...the strongest and wisest novel I have ever read about the problem of child abuse. A novel, not a polemic or tract, the book is impossible to read without being moved to fury and tears."

Author Biography

Susan Palwick lives in New Jersey, where she is currently working on her second novel. After receiving her B.A. in Creative Writing from Princeton, she did graduate work in English at Yale. Palwick is the author of a distinguished body of short fiction, mostly published in science fiction magazines, and is the winner of SF's Rhysling Award for poetry.

Topics to Consider

1   To what extent would you say the characters in this book are portrayed in black-and-white terms? Are all the women either strong or weak (but never evil)? Are all the men either good or evil (but usually dumb)? Were you able to find any shades of gray? For example, did Emma's father have any redeeming qualities? Were you able to see a dark side to any of the female characters?

2   There are many similarities in the way Ginny and Emma were both treated by their father. Yet each girl reacted differently to being abused. How might have things been different if Emma had been the older sister?

3   Did Emma's mother treat her any differently than she treated Ginny? What did her mother learn, if anything, from Ginny's death?

4   Who played the most important role in "saving" Emma, and what was it that he or she did? What parts did others play?

5   Emma's father was sentenced to three years of therapy and community service. Do you believe that the punishment fit the crime? The judge did not want him sent to jail, believing that he might become even meaner. What was your reaction to this line of reasoning?

6   The story begins with Emma's daughter entering her "special" room and finding her secret letters to Ginny. Might this invasion of Emma's privacy have any potentially negative repercussions?

7   Describe the value of Jane's relationship to Emma. What did it mean to you when Jane said that she could hear everything in class yet she never heard the breathing?

8   Why did Emma's mother act the way she did? Did she know what was happening? Could she have suspected anything?

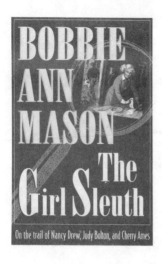

On the trail of Nancy Drew, Judy Bolton, and Cherry Ames

The Girl Sleuth

Author:
Bobbie Ann Mason

Publisher:
The University of Georgia Press

First printing: 1975
Second printing: 1995

Available in:
Quality Paper, 160 pages. $10.95
(ISBN 0-8203-1739-X)

Summary

In this new edition of a long out-of-print work, **Bobbie Ann Mason** reminisces about her childhood reading of the girl detective series books, including Nancy Drew, Judy Bolton, and Cherry Ames. Mason's recollections of a rural youth spent longing for mysteries to solve represent a quintessential American girlhood experience. *The Girl Sleuth* is a book for anyone who fondly recalls late-night adventures inside a bedspread cave with a flashlight, a handful of snitched cookies, and a savvy heroine who has just two chapters left in which to decode the message, find the jewels, unmask the impostor, and then catch the next express to the big city.

Recommended by Janice Radway

"Indispensable to the history of women's reading in the U.S. Mason is observant, funny, and opinionated when it comes to her girlhood reading."

Author Biography

Bobbie Ann Mason is the author of *Feather Crowns* (winner of the 1994 Southern Book Critics Circle Award for Fiction), *In Country*, *Shiloh and Other Stories*, *Love Life: Stories*, and *Spence + Lila*. She resides in Kentucky. *The Girl Sleuth* was her first book.

Topics to Consider

1   Did you read series books as a child and, if so, which ones? Who introduced you to them and what did your parents think of the books? Do you still have your old books?

2   Do you remember your favorite girl (or boy) sleuth story? Do you remember the "puzzle" and how the mystery was solved?

3   Bobbie Ann Mason says: "I'm still a girl sleuth, setting my magnifying glass onto words and images and the great mysteries of life." How did a girl (or boy) sleuth series open your eyes to the world or help you face life in a new way? Were you ever inspired to write your own adventure or did you ever pretend to be the hero or heroine?

4   What do you think about the significance of Nancy Drew's love of the traditionally male color blue? What other emblems of Nancy's independence are used throughout the series?

5   What do you think of Nancy Drew's perfectionism? Did you find it challenging and inspirational or intimidating and daunting?

6   In many ways Nancy Drew (and other series characters) has changed with the times. Are the Nancy Drew or series heroines and heroes that you knew still relevant today? How so?

7   In her new preface, Mason says that these stories "propelled her childhood, a kind of childhood that in its particulars is disappearing in America now." In what ways do you think childhood in America has changed? Why do you think the girl (and boy) sleuth series books have stood the test of time and still have a loyal audience today despite many social changes? If you have children, do they read series books? Which are their favorites?

8   Mysteries (and an interest in crime) seem to be more popular than ever. What do you think is behind the interest in mysteries for adults and children alike?

Girlfriends

Invisible Bonds, Enduring Ties

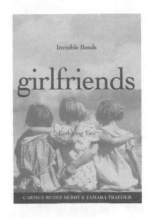

Authors:
Carmen Renee Berry
and Tamara Traeder

Publisher: Wildcat Canyon Press

First printing: 1995

Available in:
Quality Paper, 240 pages. $12.95
(ISBN 1-885171-08-0)

Summary

Almost any woman will tell you that her friendships with other women are among the most important relationships in her life. Girlfriends make us laugh, listen to us cry, tell us the truth — even when it's hard to hear — and stand up for us when necessary. Our girlfriends sometimes know us better than we know ourselves, and they understand us when no one else does. Authors **Carmen Renee Berry** and **Tamara Traeder** interviewed over a hundred women for this book. The stories collected about women and their friends are woven into essays, each of which focuses on a different aspect of friendship, including first meetings, loyalty, humor, acceptance, betrayal, forgiveness and strength. The book closes with a section of rituals or traditions, ranging from funny to serious, which women may use to celebrate their own friendships.

Recommended by *USA Today*

"Women...need to make connections with other women who understand what they face and with longtime friends who know their stories."

Author Biography

Real-life girlfriends **Carmen Renee Berry** and **Tamara Traeder** wrote this book to acknowledge and examine the central role their girlfriends play in their lives. Carmen is a best-selling author, noted speaker and former psychotherapist who lives in Pasadena, California. Tamara is a publisher and attorney who resides in Berkeley, California. They both count their friends among their greatest blessings.

READING GROUP CHOICES

Topics to Consider

1 This is a book about women's friendships. Is there any implication that men and women can't share an equally close friendship?

2 There are a number of current movies and television shows about women and their friends such as *Waiting to Exhale* and *How to Make an American Quilt.* To what do you attribute their popularity?

3 Do you believe that all women feel "warm and fuzzy" about their women friends? Don't women betray each other as well?

4 In the back of the book there is a section on women's rituals that goes beyond gossip and shopping. What rituals are important in women's relationships? Why?

5 The old rhyme says that girls are "sugar and spice and everything nice"; yet the book asserts that making trouble together is a valuable aspect of friendship for young girls and women. Do you agree? Explain.

6 Do you think that women have trouble being honest with each other? Are some circumstances more conducive to dishonesty than others?

7 What are the secrets to maintaining long friendships? Which of your friends have you known the longest? What sustains the relationship?

8 How do friendships change when one of the friends gets married or involved romantically with someone?

9 Do women fight differently than men? In what ways?

10 Do you find the title "girlfriends" offensive? Do you think it would be offensive to some women? Why or why not?

Growing Season

A Healing Journey into the Heart of Nature

Author:
Arlene Bernstein

Publisher: Wildcat Canyon Press

First printing: 1995

Available in:
Quality Paper, 180 pages. $11.95
(ISBN 1-885171-10-2)

Summary

Like other young women of her era, **Arlene Bernstein** grew up with the expectation that she would one day be a mother, and that role would be the defining factor of her identity. After the painful loss of three children and the resulting grief, Arlene came to understand that the life she had dreamed for herself would not be hers. With this realization, she began a healing process that allowed her to accept and simply live the life that was hers. Through her intimate connection to the land, Arlene learns to observe "what is" without judgment, and to live life as an active meditation. Through the power of meditative attention, she discovers that what we need the most is usually right in front of us — if only we see it differently.

Recommended by Thomas Moore

"... the earth is our best teacher, as Arlene Bernstein discovers quite naturally and writes about with beautiful candor...I recommend it in the same spirit that I would suggest making soup from your own garden."

Author Biography

Arlene Bernstein is a licensed psychotherapist and exhibiting photographer. She has presented training seminars for bereavement counselors, taught meditation and facilitated women's retreats, all based on the principles discovered in her garden and vineyard. She and her husband Michael established Mount Veeder Winery in the hills above Napa, California in the early 1970s, which they sold after building it into a successful company. After an absence of some time, she returned to the country last year to plant a new garden.

Topics to Consider

1 What did Arlene learn in her garden that allowed her to eventually renew her participation in and love of life?

2 Marriages frequently break up after the partners experience great tragedy in their lives. We know from reading this book that Arlene considered leaving Michael. What made her stay?

3 What was Arlene's experience of the grief "process"? What is yours?

4 How did Arlene find an outlet for the creative energy she thought would be for her children? How might you have responded in a similar situation?

5 Have you ever had the experience of a turning point (pages 23-25), being still, empty, open, and had an answer just pop into your consciousness? What do you call that experience? Inspiration, intuition or God?

6 Arlene says to Michael, "Our first marriage is dead, but I'd just as soon you be my second husband" (page 63). What has been your experience with stages in relationships? What communication is necessary for relationships to restructure rather than come apart?

7 Referring to the passage about Swiss chard (pages 82-83), do you recognize the dynamic of becoming devious and manipulative or exhibiting other negative traits when you don't feel heard and acknowledged? How does this story illustrate the bind that old conditioning creates when we try to live our present lives based on past rules?

8 Throughout the book, Arlene relates her own development to the changing of the seasons, the cyclical way that life itself unfolds. How do you see life, death, and renewal interacting in your own life? Do you tend to resist the inevitable nature of change, or do you let yourself learn anew with each fresh cycle?

9 What do you consider your "garden" — the physical or mental place you go for peace and inspiration?

The Heat of the Sun

LOUIS D. RUBIN, JR.

Author:
Louis D. Rubin, Jr.

Publisher: Longstreet Press

First printing: 1995

Available in:
Hardcover, 448 pages. $21.95
(ISBN 1-56352-233-0)

Summary

This tale of romance, mystery and intrigue transports the reader to Charleston, South Carolina, 1940.   Mike Quinn, a rookie newspaper reporter, has come to Charleston to be near his fiancee, Betsy Murray, daughter of a local developer and power broker. As their relationship unravels and Mike discovers the truth about Betsy's past, he also uncovers the truth about her father's sordid business deals. Meanwhile, on the campus of the College of Charleston, a different sort of scandal is brewing over the surprise appointment of a new dean. Louis Rubin seamlessly weaves these two storylines together, along with a delightful cast of secondary characters, still another intrigue about a mysterious boat, and illuminating tales about sea turtles, Civil War batteries, and the nautical world.

Recommended by Clyde Edgerton

"...a very funny yet deeply moving novel."

Author Biography

Louis D. Rubin, Jr., the founder of Algonquin Books of Chapel Hill and a founding member of the Fellowship of Southern Writers, taught English and creative writing for many years. He has written or edited some 45 books, the most recent of which are *The Edge of the Swamp, Small Craft Advisory, The Mockingbird in the Gum Tree,* and *A Writer's Companion.* He lives in Chapel Hill, North Carolina, and in his spare time pursues his interests in painting, boating, military history, and baseball.

Topics to Consider

1   What is the significance of the novel's title, taken from Shakespeare's *Cymbeline*?

2   The two principal characters in the book, Rosy and Mike, are both "outsiders," although Rosy is a native of Charleston. Discuss the different as well as similar reasons for their outsider relationship with the city.

3   How do the elaborate politics of campus life at the College of Charleston serve as a thread to connect various elements of the story?

4   Discuss the role of nature in the novel. In what ways does the author use nature to contribute to the development of his characters?

5   The attempt to ban Andrew Marvel's *To His Coy Mistress* is as relevant today as it was in 1940. How does this incident serve as a turning point for both Rosy and Mike?

6   How do you feel about the resolution of the Ghost Ship mystery? Why don't Rosy and Sara Jane reveal what they learn?

7   The final chapter of the novel lets us see what became of the various characters in the years ahead. Were there any surprises or disappointments for you? If so, what would you like to have turned out differently?

8   The novel is full of funny and interesting people. Who was your favorite character? Why?

9   Taken as a whole, what does the novel have to say about human nature?

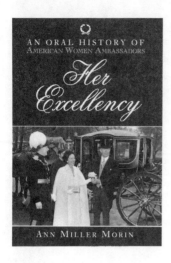

Her Excellency

An Oral History of American Women Ambassadors

Author:
Ann Miller Morin

Publisher: Twayne/Macmillan

First printing: 1995

Available in:
Quality Paper, 315 pages. $16.95
(ISBN 0-8057-9142-6)
Hardcover, 315 pages. $27.95
(ISBN 0-8057-9118-3)

Summary

A chance encounter with a former colleague who had become America's thirteenth woman ambassador led **Ann Miller Morin** to embark on a ten-year study of the distaff side of U. S. diplomacy-at-the-top. She began her work by recording oral histories of 34 of the 36 then-living female ambassadors. Using several criteria, fifteen of these documents were carefully selected and these, buttressed by archival research and more than 150 interviews with colleagues and supervisors, present an eloquent account of the vivid events these high achievers experienced and the obstacles they overcame in succeeding in a traditional male preserve. This unique work conveys to the reader what it is like to be an ambassador who also happens to be a woman.

Recommended by Senator Nancy Landon Kassebaum

"The achievements of women are not often found in history books, and your account will help fill a void...."

Author Biography

Ann Miller Morin has pursued her profession as a writer and educator throughout a peripatetic life as wife of a Foreign Service Officer. In addition to her responsibilities as a diplomatic hostess, she taught at U.S. Army schools in France and Japan and was principal of international schools in Iraq and Algeria. A graduate of the Universities of New Hampshire (BA) and Maryland (MA), she writes for journals of diplomacy and oral history.

Topics to Consider

1   What did you learn about life in the Foreign Service from this book? What did you find most surprising?

2   The husbands of ambassadors are in a difficult position because they must take a back seat to their wives. Do you believe most American husbands would be comfortable in such a situation? How did the husbands discussed in this book handle the relationship? Which strategies were most successful?

3   What personal characteristics did these women share that enabled them to overcome the resistance all women encounter in advancing in a male-dominated profession?

4   The majority of political appointees came from careers either in politics or in academia. Which do you think provides the better training or background for the diplomatic service? Explain.

5   In what ways does the sex of the ambassador influence how he or she is regarded in the host country? Do these factors affect the degree of success of a given envoy?

6   Male ambassadors depend a great deal on their wives for assistance and support: entertaining, managing the residence, doing volunteer work, and maintaining social relations with wives of local officials. Not having the equivalent of a "wife," women ambassadors are at a disadvantage. What would you suggest as ways to overcome this lack?

7   Do you believe that personal wealth is desirable or necessary to being an ambassador? Is U. S. prestige damaged if an ambassador cannot provide lavish entertainment?

8   Of the career ambassadors discussed in the book, only one had biological children, while all of the political ambassadors were mothers. What was there about the Foreign Service career that resulted in such a dramatic difference between the two groups?

9   Do you agree with the author's conclusions about future prospects for women who wish to pursue careers in diplomacy? Why or why not?

How We Die

Reflections on Life's Final Chapter

Author:
Sherwin B. Nuland

Publisher: Vintage Books

First printing: 1994

Available in:
Quality Paper, 304 pages. $13.00
(ISBN 0-679-74244-1)

Summary

There is a vast literature on death and dying, but there are few reliable accounts of the ways in which we die. The intimate account of how various diseases take away life, offered in *How We Die*, is not meant to prompt horror or terror but to demythologize the process of dying, to help us rid ourselves of the fear of death. **Sherwin Nuland** explores the seven most common roads to death and how we shall die, each of us in a way that will be unique. He tells what will happen through particular stories of dying — of patients, of his own family — and shows us some of the facets of death's multiplicity. At once a memoir and meditation, biological and therapeutic guide, *How We Die* is a book unlike any other.

Recommended by Oliver Sacks

"As powerful and sensitive, and unsparing and unsentimental as anything I have ever read."

Author Biography

Sherwin B. Nuland is the author of *Doctors: The Biography of Medicine,* as well as *The Origins of Anasthesia,* a volume in the Classics of Medicine Library. Chairman of the Board of Managers of the *Journal of the History of Medicine and Allied Sciences* and literary editor of *Connecticut Medicine,* he teaches surgery and the history of medicine at Yale University.

Topics to Consider

1   Why does the author call the idea of "a good death" a myth? If he is correct, are we any better off knowing that it is a myth?

2   Does the author believe that we should approach death and disease in different ways? How does he distinguish between the two?

3   In his introduction, Nuland says that his intention is "to demythologize the process of dying." Does he accomplish this purpose? How does he treat this goal with respect to the specific "doors" to death? Does his writing create different attitudes toward different diseases?

4   What was your emotional reaction to this book? Was it different from what you might have expected?

5   How would Nuland describe a good doctor? A good patient? Would the condition being treated alter his descriptions?

6   Why does Nuland consider medicine to be more art than science?

7   The author believes that life has "natural, inherent limits." How is this belief reflected in his attitudes toward old age and euthanasia? Do you agree?

8   In the process of dying, where does Nuland find dignity? Where does he find hope? Is faith a part of his picture? In what way?

9   How might this book have changed any of your ideas or expectations about death and dying?

The Hundred Secret Senses

Author:
Amy Tan

Publisher: G.P. Putnam's Sons

First printing: 1995

Available in:
Hardcover, 368 pages. $23.95
(ISBN 0-399-14114-6)

Summary

Olivia is only five years old when Kwan, her seventeen-year-old half sister from China, moves into her bedroom and turns her world upside down. Olivia, who wants only to lead a normal American life, tries to chase Kwan's secrets and ghost stories from her imagination. For thirty years, Olivia endures visits from Kwan and her ghosts, who appear to offer advice on everything from restaurants to Olivia's failed marriage. When unexpected circumstances bring her, her estranged husband, and Kwan together in the mountain village of Kwan's childhood, Olivia finds a way to reconcile the ghosts of her past with the dreams of her future. A series of secrets unfold that question the connections between chance and fate, beliefs and hopes, memory and imagination, and the natural gifts of our hundred secret senses.

Recommended by *Newsweek*

"...a wonderful writer with a rare power to touch the heart."

Author Biography

Amy Tan was born in Oakland, California in 1952, and grew up in the San Francisco Bay area. She graduated from high school in Switzerland, and received her Master's degree in linguistics from San Jose State University. Tan is the author of *The Joy Luck Club, The Kitchen God's Wife,* and two books for children. She has been married for 21 years, and lives in San Francisco and New York with her husband, a cat named Sagwa, and dog, Mr. Zo.

Topics to Consider

1   Throughout the novel, Olivia resists the love, the stories, and the Yin eyes of her half-sister, Kwan. Why is she so resistant? When does she accept Kwan's Yin eyes and her stories?

2   How does Olivia's relationship with her mother and her early loss of her father affect her relationship with Kwan? With her husband, Simon?

3   What is the significance of Olivia's career as a photographer? What does it show about her feelings toward her memory? How does she use her camera to connect with people and events?

4   How do lies, promises, friendship and love bind people through more than one lifetime in *The Hundred Secret Senses*? How do they break down the boundaries between the past and the present?

5   What does the story about Kwan's childhood death by drowning with a girl named Buncake say about identity? How does Olivia react to the story?

6   On page 357, Olivia says "truth lies not in logic but in hope, both past and future." What does she mean by this? How does she arrive at this conclusion? Do you agree with her?

7   Do you think Kwan is fated to disappear in China? Why or why not?

8   How does Olivia change because of the events that take place in China?

I Speak For This Child
True Stories of a Child Advocate

Author:
Gay Courter

Publisher: Crown

First printing: 1995

Available in:
Quality Paper, 416 pages. $15.00
(ISBN 0-517-88686-3)

Summary

Every day, children are entangled — often as the victims of neglect or abuse — in legal proceedings they can't comprehend but that greatly affect their chances for future security and happiness. In a system where parents are represented by lawyers, social workers are hampered by bureaucratic rules, and judges must remain impartial, only the Guardian ad Litem speaks directly on behalf of the children. This is the true story of **Gay Courter's** work as a Guardian: of the legal powers, responsibilities, and duties her position entailed; of her fierce efforts to ensure that her clients were treated with care and respect; and of the rewards of participating in this nationwide volunteer program.

Recommended by the *San Francisco Chronicle*

"A fascinating and disturbing insider's look at the children lost in the legal shuffle and foster care system ... and the difference one person's efforts can make."

Author Biography

Gay Courter is the author of *The Midwife, The Midwife's Advice, Flowers in the Blood,* and other best-selling novels. In *I Speak For This Child,* she recounts her experiences as a Guardian ad Litem, a court-appointed advocate for children involved in the legal system.

Topics to Consider

1   Why does society seem to be uncomfortable and reluctant to place the interests of children above the interests of their parents?

2   Were you familiar with the Guardian Ad Litem program prior to reading this book? What do believe to be the flaws and strengths of this program?

3   Which of the several models that the author presents for representing children's needs in legal proceedings (page 349) seem to speak best for the child in court? Do any other models come to mind? Why not leave child advocacy to paid professionals?

4   Why are children removed from the decision-making process especially when these decisions directly impact their lives and futures? Should a child's views be more intrinsically valued? Why or why not?

5   What are your feelings about states' involvement in family matters? Where should the line be drawn?

6   Why do the services established to help children seem to work independently and often in opposition to one another? What can be done to create open lines of communication between organizations that allegedly have the same goal(s) — serving the best interests of the child — in mind?

7   What are your feelings about the distinctions between primary and secondary parental rights (page 362) and the open adoption that this structure would facilitate? Discuss potential problems with this approach.

*If I had my life
to live over*
I would pick more daisies

If I had
my life to live over
I would pick more daisies

Editor:
Sandra Haldeman Martz

Publisher: Papier-Mache

First printing: 1992

Available in:
Quality Paper, 205 pages. $10.00
(ISBN 0-918949-24-6)
Hardcover, 205 pages. $18.00
(ISBN 0-918949-25-4)

Summary

This anthology focuses on the decisions, public and private, that shape women's lives. Inspired by the title poem in which an older woman looks back on a life sensibly lived and wishes she had "eaten more ice cream and less beans," editor **Sandra Martz** has brought together stories, poems, and photographs that "cut across a spectrum of age, race and ways of life." This rich collection offers a rare opportunity for readers to listen to women's voices speaking about life issues and choices that matter most to them.

Recommended by the *Los Angeles Times*

"A genuine, gentle reminder that it's never too late to change."

Editor Biography

Frustrated with the lack of creativity in her corporate job, **Sandra Haldeman Martz** worked after hours on her book projects in her garage. She realized that she touched a chord with *When I Am an Old Woman I Shall Wear Purple*. Five years and one million copies later, she edited and published this companion volume. The philosophy that guides Martz's selections is accessibility. She has earned a unique reputation as representing the emotions and experiences of women everywhere.

Topics to Consider

1   What are some of the choices made by the women in this book? How did it affect their lives? What led them to make these decisions?

2   Are there certain decisions that all women make at particular times in their lives?

3   What missed opportunities are recounted? And what can we learn from them?

4   If you had your life to live over, are there some things you would do differently?

5   How has gender and ethnicity affected the choices these women have made?

6   Some of these poems and stories imply an urgency to life, without a moment to waste. Do you agree with this feeling? Why or why not?

7   What is one decision, small or large, that significantly affected your life?

8   How do you feel about the women's voices and experiences represented in the collection? Which women in the book did you connect with?

9   Would men make different decisions than women? How would their decisions be different?

Lifecycles

Jewish Women on Life Passages & Personal Milestones (Volume 1)

Editor:
Rabbi Debra Orenstein

Publisher: Jewish Lights Publishing

First printing: 1994

Available in:
Hardcover, 432 pages. $24.95
(ISBN 1-879045-14-1)

Summary

Recent years have seen an explosion of interest in personal ritual and spirituality, as well as an exciting expansion of women's participation and leadership in Jewish life. This volume brings together over 50 women writers, rabbis, and scholars to create the first comprehensive work on Jewish life cycle that fully includes women's perspectives. In a style that is perceptive and passionate, insightful and personal, *Lifecycles Vol. 1* covers the spectrum of life's passages and personal milestones – Childbirth, Conversion, Marriage, Singlehood, Coming Out, Mid-Life, Divorce, Aging and more. The contributors explore tradition and innovation, and express the way women see – and affect – the world. Introductions by **Rabbi Debra Orenstein** provide readers with a broader context for the ideas shared in each section.

Recommended by Letty Cottin Pogrebin

"Nothing is missing from this marvelous collection. You will turn to it for rituals and inspiration, prayer and poetry, comfort and community. Lifecycles is a gift to the Jewish woman in America."

Editor Biography

Rabbi Debra Orenstein, editor of the *Lifecycles* series, is a popular author and teacher of Judaism, spirituality and gender studies. She is a Senior Fellow of the Wilstein Institute of Jewish Policy Studies and an instructor at the University of Judaism in Los Angeles. A seventh generation rabbi, she was in the first rabbinical school class at the Jewish Theological Seminary to include women.

Topics to Consider

1 How does ritual help individuals and society function? Is there a danger or downside to creative ritual? Do you agree with the characterization of the impetus of ritual (pp. xx-xxi)? With Whitmont's statement quoted on p. 124?

2 Choose a topic or occasion around which you wish to create a new ritual and/or prayer. (This can be something of interest to the group alone, or the group can tackle a situation that involves the larger community.) Use the Afterword as a guide. What unexpected issues/problems arise in forming your ritual?

3 How do the contrasting voices in the chapter on Adolescence resonate with this subject? What understanding do you remember from your own life about struggling with religious and gender issues during adolescence?

4 Chapter 7 and "Uncharted Territory" (p. 173) offer insights about the emotions involved in Jewish lesbian identity. How might the experience of "coming out" as a lesbian apply to all women? To all Jews? (See pp. 142-143.)

5 In the chapter on "Invisible Life Passages" in particular, how effective are the authors of the rituals at marking — and creating awareness of — life passages many people have never considered?

6 What do the writings — for example, pp. 121-122, Chapters 2, 15, and the Click Story by Holub (p. 378) — say about the relationship between personal and communal suffering/ mourning? Is it desirable to personalize communal suffering, and conversely, to render our personal tragedies communally relevant?

7 What are the contrasts among the authors writing about aging? Which of these perspectives best resonates with your experience? Discuss matriphobia, the idea of filling one's mother's shoes, and your personal experience with aging, or with your aging mother.

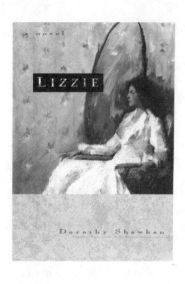

Lizzie

Author:
Dorothy Shawhan

Publisher: Longstreet Press

First printing: 1995

Available in:
Hardcover, 352 pages. $20.00
(ISBN 1-56352-227-6)

Summary

Based on the life of a governor's daughter born in 1902, *Lizzie* is the story of a brilliant yet tragic woman who struggles to find her place — in a Southern world of conflicting values, under the rule of a father who psychologically destroys everyone around him. Readers will be spellbound by the interwoven storylines, a journey through women's suffrage, Jim Crow, and the Depression, overlaid with an antique dealer's tussle over the Dunbar family papers. **Dorothy Shawhan** captures the voices of this volatile era — Lizzie's childhood nanny, Tennessee Williams, and others who were struck by her explosive mixture of Southern charm and progressive politics.

Recommended by Lee Smith

"You can't take your eyes off of wild, beautiful Lizzie Dunbar as she waltzes recklessly through the whole history of the Deep South in a tragic bravura performance."

Author Biography

Dorothy Shawhan teaches English and journalism at Delta State University in Cleveland, Mississippi, and is chair of the Division of Languages and Literature. *Lizzie* is her first novel.

Topics to Consider

1   The story of *Lizzie* is told by a medley of voices, mixing the past and the present. How might the story have been different if it were told entirely from Lizzie's perspective?

2   Though we never directly hear Mrs. Cavanaugh's voice, how does her character most clearly convey the convergence of past and present?

3   To what extent can the tragedy of Lizzie's life be attributed to the times in which she lived? Her own personal weaknesses? How might Lizzie's life have been different if she were living in the 1990s?

4   Lizzie says at one point that her father gave her "every opportunity". Do you agree? To what extent is Lizzie's relationship with Stephen to blame for the tragic turn her life took?

5   The story focuses on Lizzie, yet we also experience the suffering of several other characters throughout the book. What is the author's purpose in showing us this accumulation of pain?

6   What do the historical characters (e.g. Tennessee Williams, William Faulkner) contribute to the story?

7   At the end of the book, Meems says "We can't judge the worth of a life ... Who can know what other lives it touches and how it contributes to the flow?" Discuss the many ways Lizzie's life touched others and "contributed to the flow."

8   Would you have liked to know Lizzie? What would your relationship with her have been like?

Mother Journeys
Feminists Write about Mothering

Editors:
Maureen T. Reddy, Martha Roth,
Amy Sheldon

Publisher: Spinsters Ink
First printing: 1994
Available in:
Quality Paper, 352 pages. $15.95
(ISBN 0-883523-03-6)
Hardcover, 352 pages. $29.95
(ISBN 0-883523-04-4)

Summary

Winner of a 1995 Minnesota Book Award and a 1995 Susan Koppelman Award by the Women's Caucus of the Popular Culture Association and the American Culture Association, *Mother Journeys* is a compelling collection of essays, stories, poems, and artwork investigating with clarity, humor, courage, and sometimes pain, the dual issues of motherhood and feminism. Employing both words and images, feminist mothers write about abortion, infertility, miscarriages, the death of a child. They also explore the sensual joys of mothering, the intellectual joy of discovering another person's growth, and, ultimately, how their personal and political identities are shaped by raising children.

Recommended by Sara Ruddick

"...A glimpse of what mothering might become when illumined by feminist consciousness. A wonderful book!"

Editors' Biography

Maureen T. Reddy is an associate professor of English and director of the Women's Studies Program at Rhode Island College. She has also written *Crossing the Color Line: Race, Parenting and Culture* (Rutgers, 1995). Minneapolis resident **Martha Roth** is founding editor of *Hurricane Alice: A Feminist Quarterly* and a co-editor of *Transforming a Rape Culture* (Milkweed, 1993). Her first novel, *Goodness*, will be published by Spinsters Ink in the Spring of 1996. **Amy Sheldon** is a professor of linguistics and feminist studies at the University of Minnesota.

Topics to Consider

1 Is there a difference between being a mother and a feminist mother?

2 What exactly is a "real mom" as described on page 71? For you, who is the "*real* mom who lives in your head?"

3 What are some of the ways in which motherhood emotionally and physically changes women's lives?

4 What are some of the authors' preconceived notions about what motherhood would be like?

5 According to Judith Arcana, in what way is abortion a motherhood issue?

6 Throughout *Mother Journeys*, what are some of the authors' concerns regarding the medical community's attitude towards childbirth?

7 On page 303, Molly Collins Layton asks, "What is the mother to do with her cynicism, her irony, her urge to throw the dinner plates against the fence?" What does society demand from mothers? Why is the Norman Rockwell interpretation of motherhood so popular?

8 How does Martha Roth go about giving her children the freedom to make their own life choices without compromising her feminist principles?

9 What does Barbara Schapiro mean when she writes that motherhood has thrust her into a "state of negative capability?"

10 In what ways can choosing to have children enrich a woman's life and be a positive component of a feminist lifestyle?

Old Dogs and Children

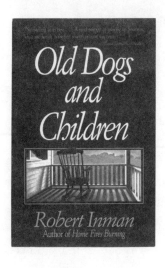

Author:
Robert Inman

Publisher: Little, Brown and Co.

First printing: 1991

Available in:
Quality Paper, 456 pages. $10.95
(ISBN 0-316-41914-1)

Summary

Weaving together past and present, *Old Dogs and Children* introduces us to four generations of the Bascombe clan and to its strong-willed and compassionate matriarch, Bright Birdsong. When a series of family and community crises (a tragic accident that ignites old racial tensions, a visit from her estranged daughter, a scandal involving her son the governor and a local cocktail waitress) shatters her calm, she has a once-in-a-lifetime opportunity to right old wrongs and to reconcile who she has become with who she wants to be.

Recommended by the *Atlanta Journal/Constitution*

"Storytelling at its best ... A vivid portrait of growing up Southern, white and female in the first seventy years of this century."

Author Biography

Robert Inman, the author of *Home Fire Burning*, is an Alabama native and a University of Alabama graduate. He lives in Charlotte, North Carolina, where he works as a television anchorman. He is married to Paulette; they have two daughters.

Topics to Consider

1 How does Bright Bascombe Birdsong identify with the images of old dogs and children? What characteristics do old dogs and children share with an aging white Southern woman?

2 The mother (Elise), father (Dorsey), daughter (Bright) triangle has tragic consequences. Does Elise make Dorsey choose between herself and their daughter? How is each character responsible for creating this destructive triangle?

3 Within the pages of *Old Dogs and Children*, there is much discussion of an individual's quest for identity. How does one achieve "identity"? Is it linked to one's family? One's place? Or one's perceived responsibilities?

4 How do the elements of sun and water shape Bright's past, present and future? What does she take from these elements? What do they take from her? And what, if anything, do they give her in return?

5 Discuss Bright's relationship with Flavo. Why does she seem to side with him on issues which pit her against her husband and her son?

6 The most important events in Bright's life are marked by either a profound presence or profound lack of music. What causes Bright to lose her internal music? How does she regain it?

7 Bright's senses of sound and smell are crucial in helping her interpret her world. How does she use these senses to retreat from the world, and conversely, to reaffirm her presence in the world and in her town?

8 Explain why Bright refuses to relocate to Washington, D.C. even after her father dies. What choices, if any, did you make in living where you do?

9 Discuss the similarities that exist between Roseann and Elise. What effect does this have in their relationships with Bright?

Revelation

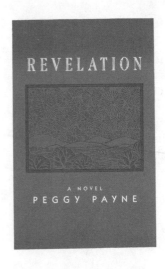

Author:
Peggy Payne

Publisher: Banks Channel Books

First printing: 1988

Available in:
Quality Paper, 315 pages. $12.95
(ISBN 0-9635967-1-3)

Summary

Revelation is a powerful and disturbing novel about Swain Hammond, a Presbyterian minister in Chapel Hill, North Carolina, who stands in his backyard one summer evening waiting for dinner to cook on the grill — and suddenly, literally, hears the voice of God. His wife thinks he's having a stroke. His liberal, academic congregation thinks he's crazy. As Swain tries to deal with the presence of the holy in a skeptical, secular world, he finds himself behaving in unexpected and emotional ways, especially after a boy is tragically blinded during a church clean-up day. Swain's struggle is both wrenching and painful, yet it leaves him a better minister and a better man. This is a probing tale of revelation, spiritual growth, and redemption in modern times.

Recommended by *the Atlanta Journal/Constitution*

"...Real emotional power ... most readers will find themselves both satisfied and disturbed."

Author Biography

Peggy Payne is the co-author of the nonfiction book, *The Healing Power of Doing Good.* Her fiction has been cited in *Best American Short Stories* and included in *New Stories of the South.* She is also a travel writer and journalist whose articles have appeared in national newspapers and magazines ranging from *Cosmopolitan* and *Travel and Leisure* to *The Mother Earth News* and *The Washington Post.* She lives near Chapel Hill, North Carolina.

Topics to Consider

1   In the beginning, Swain feels that as a minister he is under pressure, particularly among other ministers, to "act like Captain Kangaroo," i.e. to present himself as warm and sensitive. He has chosen a church where this kind of expectation will be minimal. Do people have unrealistic expectations of ministers? If so, what are they? What is the result?

2   Swain is particularly hesitant to tell people in his church about hearing the voice because they are a group with a strong intellectual bent. How might intellect interfere with spirituality?

3   If you were sitting in a pew and the minister got up and claimed to have heard God speaking in his backyard, would you believe it? Or would you, like the people in Swain's church, recommend psychotherapy?

4   Believers are often comfortable with the idea of miraculous happenings occurring in the very distant past, but not now. Why then and not now? What role, if any, does the downfall of several popular televangelists play in what people choose to believe?

5   At the close of the story Julie and Swain are expecting a baby. Swain has resolved, after so much reluctance, to do the best he can. What kind of father will Swain be?

6   If Swain and Julie were friends of yours, would you have expected their marriage to last?

7   Does Swain make you mad? If so, why?

8   Childhood loneliness and the desire for magic are the reasons that Swain gives for his earliest thoughts of becoming a minister. Much New Age spirituality focuses on what used to be considered the occult or magic. Why is the desire for magic occurring so strongly now?

9   Did Swain hear God? Or not? What makes you think so?

Rhoda
A Life in Stories

Author:
Ellen Gilchrist

Publisher: Little, Brown and Co.

First printing: 1995

Available in:
Quality Paper, 464 pages. $13.95
(ISBN 0-316-31464-1)

Summary

With a raging libido and reckless courage to match, Rhoda is one of those irresistible people who never hold back and never take convention too seriously. From a precocious kid with a movie-star complex and a coed who elopes with a fraternity boy to a middle-aged writer looking for an AIDS-free fling, here is all of Rhoda in all her wicked glory. This volume offers a complete retrospective collection of stories, plus two new ones, featuring everyone's favorite Ellen Gilchrist character — Rhoda Katherine Manning.

Recommended by Robert Olen Butler

"Rhoda's feisty, sexy, and devastatingly acute sensibilities make her one of the most engaging and surprisingly lovable characters in modern fiction."

Author Biography

Ellen Gilchrist was born in Vicksburg, Mississippi, and as a child moved many times with her family to other cities in the South and Midwest. She studied writing with Eudora Welty, and published her first book in 1979. She is the critically acclaimed author of eleven previous books, including the National Book Award-winning *Victory Over Japan* and, most recently, *The Age of Miracles*. For readers who wonder how much of Rhoda is autobiographical, Gilchrist drops some hints in her introduction. The mother of three grown sons, she currently lives near Fayetteville, Arkansas.

Topics to Consider

1   Gilchrist has been writing about Rhoda for years, but this is the first time all of Rhoda can be found in one place. What kind of discrepancies are there in her life story? How does she evolve, and how does she stay notably the same?

2   Rhoda's indomitable libido is one of her most notable characteristics. How does her relationship with men affect her life? Who controls whom? How complex are her male characters in this respect, or Rhoda for that matter?

3   Family plays a large part of Rhoda's life. Does she ultimately want to escape from her parents and siblings, or does she cherish her family ties? Or both? How does Rhoda's relationship with her family of origin compare to the complex feelings she has toward her own children?

4   What does Rhoda's disillusionment about marriage teach her about herself? About her family? Do you think her experiences reflect those of other women who came of age in the 1950s? How do they speak to women's experiences today?

5   Discuss the difference between love and respect. Which is more important to Rhoda and her family?

6   Gilchrist has said that writing "is more like memory than imagination." Discuss the importance of memories — especially memories of childhood and family.

The Romance Reader

Author:
Pearl Abraham

Publisher: Riverhead

First printing: 1995

Available in:
Hardcover, 304 pages. $21.95
(ISBN 1-57322-015-9)

Summary

This novel allows us to enter the Chassidic community through the life of a young girl on the brink of adulthood. Rachel Benjamin is the daughter of a visionary rabbi who dreams of building a synagogue. As the rabbi's eldest daughter, Rachel is expected to set an exemplary role for her five siblings and for the community: amongst other prohibitions, she is not to read books in English. Rachel is a dreamer like her father; but her dreams are of the strong, confident men and the beautiful damsels-in-distress she reads about in the romance novels she sneaks under her blankets at night. While her mother is in Israel and her father is on the road, she craves the independence she will never have as a Chassidic woman in an arranged marriage. As her betrothal draws near, the pulls of family and faith weigh against the frightening and unknown "other" world beyond hers.

Recommended by Daphne Merkin

"...Lifts the veil on the sealed-off world of ultra-Orthodox Jews. Abraham's novel marks the debut of an enormously gifted and original writer."

Author Biography

Pearl Abraham grew up in a Chassidic community in upstate New York. She teaches English at St. Anne's School in Brooklyn. This is her first book.

Topics to Consider

1 Rachel repeatedly takes on the role of motherhood during the novel, most significantly when her mother goes to Israel. How do these responsibilities affect Rachel's attitude toward growing up and getting married?

2 At first, Rachel's mother is constantly complaining that she is miserable. How do her complaints affect Rachel? Do you think Rachel is acting out her mother's desires when she rebels against her?

3 Rachel faces many restrictions in the Chassidic world because she is a woman. How does this affect her relationship with the men in her family? With men outside her family? With other women?

4 How does Rachel's rebellion against the rules in her family differ from her sister Leah's? Where does this difference stem from? Are there any signs that Rachel's other siblings will follow her lead?

5 Describe Rachel's relationship with and feelings toward Chassidism. What factors contribute to her feeling the way she does?

6 Why does Rachel decide to marry Israel?

7 Rachel makes certain sacrifices during her marriage: shaving her hair, wearing a head scarf. Why does she make these sacrifices? What effect do they have on her marriage? Do you think she ever really wants the marriage to work?

8 Why does Rachel return home at the end of the book? How has her relationship to her family changed? What do you think the ending indicates about Rachel's future?

9 What is the significance of the book's title?

10 Are Rachel's experiences in the Chassidic world relevant to secular experiences of coming-of-age? In what ways do you identify with her? In what ways do you not?

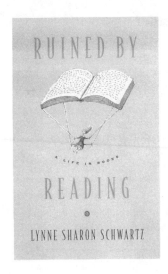

Ruined by Reading
A Life in Books

Author:
Lynne Sharon Schwartz

Publisher: Beacon Press

First printing: May, 1996

Available in:
Hardcover, 128 pages. $18.00
(ISBN 0-8070-7082-3)

Summary

The author recounts a childhood full of adventure, discovery and imagination, all within the covers of books. This book of memories concerns itself with why we read and what life we would lose without reading. By examining her own experiences of reading — from childhood to her adult life — **Lynne Schwartz** explores what reading has meant to her, and what impact on her young life specific books had. *Ruined by Reading* is not only about finding and defining oneself through reading, but also about the power of imagination and the books that shaped the world of one wonderfully imaginative reader. This book invites all readers to contemplate their own reading lives and recall what books were important to them at different times in their development as readers.

Recommended by Marcie Hershman:

"It felt as if I were having an intimate conversation — I found myself testing my own memories of reading..."

Author Biography

Lynne Sharon Schwartz is one of this country's most acclaimed novelists. When *Disturbances in the Field* was published in 1984, the New York Times praised it as "Wonderful...it goes beyond literature and philosophy to a tough, battered truth." Since then, Schwartz has written several more novels and a collection of nonfiction, including her latest work, *The Fatigue Artist.* She lives in New York City.

Topics to Consider

1   Do you recall having someone read to you as a child? Who read to you? Did you ask for the same story to be read over and over? Do you still have any of your childhood favorites?

2   How old were you when you began reading? What is the first book you remember reading?

3   Did any particular books have special significance to you in your childhood? What were the storylines?

4   What are your recollections about reading as an adolescent?

5   Have you reread any books from your childhood as an adult? Why do you think they were significant?

6   Which books have had special significance in your adult life? Share some examples of books that have been particularly meaningful. Talk about what was happening in your life at the time, and why the book(s) had such an impact.

7   Discuss the significance of this book's title. In what ways can our lives by "ruined" by reading?

Searching for Mercy Street

My Journey Back to My Mother, Anne Sexton

Author:
Linda Gray Sexton

Publisher: Little, Brown and Co.

First printing: 1994

Available in:
Quality Paper, 320 pages. $12.95
(ISBN 0-316-78208-4)

Summary

Life with Anne Sexton was a wild ride of suicidal depression and manic happiness, sexual indiscretions and midnight trips to the psychiatric ward. **Linda Sexton** was twenty-one when her mother killed herself, and now, at forty — almost the same age Anne was when she died — she looks back, remembers, and tries to come to terms with her mother's death. Anne taught Linda how to write, how to see, and how to imagine, and only Linda could have written a book that captures so vividly the intimate details and lingering emotions of their lives together.

Recommended by Susan Cheever

"Any mother or daughter, any child of an alcoholic parent ... will recognize themselves in this ravishing portrait."

Author Biography

Linda Gray Sexton is the author of four novels, including *Points of Light* and *Private Acts,* and two works of nonfiction. She lives on the West Coast with her husband and sons.

Topics to Consider

1   The author gives us an intimate view of the basic relationship of life and love gone awry. How was she able to come to understand this relationship?

2   The path to understanding and forgiveness is remembering. The author asks: "How much am I willing to endure in order to remember? Do I truly want to be empowered by memory and language?" How many of your own childhood memories were triggered by reading this book?

3   The author uses the metaphor of the "deep drawer" for the past (page 38). What other metaphors aid and assist her in remembering?

4   The demon in this book is depression. What do you understand about depression? Why is it so prevalent? What light does the author cast on this widespread social phenomenon?

5   "As time passed, [Nana] became more matriarchal, more stubborn and controlling." Consider how people you know have become what they were expected to be rather than become who they really were.

6   What constitutes "moments of normalcy" in family relations?

7   An absent father added the pressure of economic necessity to the mother/daughter relationship. Are there ways that economic necessity can have a positive family influence rather than a destructive one?

8   The author makes it clear that neither of her parents were prepared for the responsibilities of parenthood. It is also clear that getting married out of love for one another does not make the best preparation for parenthood. How can we best prepare for becoming parents?

9   The book ends with a conversation that we are not capable of having while we are growing up. What prevents us from understanding who we and those closest to us really are? How can mother and daughter become reconciled in the telling and listening of the stories that we are?

She Taught Me to Eat Artichokes

Author:
Mary Kay Shanley

Publisher: Sta-Kris, Inc.

First printing: 1993

Available in:
Hardcover, 40 pages. $13.95
(ISBN 1-882835-10-7)

Summary

In this richly illustrated story of day-to-day events, the artichoke acts as a metaphor for the growing friendship with the woman next door. Mary Kay Shanley's narrator is more inclined to buy lettuce and tomatoes and green beans — traditional, reliable, and easy to prepare when the cares of home and career are demanding. Time progresses — daily routines, a son's car accident, the Fourth of July, and winter holidays — as the neighbors slowly form a bond. Invited to a dinner party, the narrator learns how peeling one petal at a time finally uncovers the gift of the plant, just as time and effort have uncovered the rare and tender richness of the human heart.

Recommended by Fred Gacek, Village Book & Stationery

"This book — one that we suggest to our book clubs — is a wonderful story of how friendships develop. It offers insight on how people commit to one another as protective layers are peeled away."

Author Biography

Twenty-five years ago, **Mary Kay Shanley** took a temporary leave-of-absence from the *Des Moines Register* newsroom. She still hasn't made it back. She did, however, pursue her passion for writing as a freelance contributor to the *Register* as well as to numerous magazines including *Better Homes and Gardens* and *Mature Outlook*. Since 1993, Shanley has published two other books: *Little Lessons for Teachers*, and her latest book, *The Memory Box*.

Topics to Consider

1 In *She Taught Me to Eat Artichokes*, the central figure keeps ignoring artichokes in favor of lettuce, tomatoes and green beans when she is shopping. What does the author mean with this analogy? Do you also ignore artichokes in your own life?

2 It's been said that women have women friends and that men have men buddies. What's the difference between a friend and a buddy? How do men's friendships with other men differ from women's friendships with other women?

3 Do you have a childhood friend whose relationship has continued and grown through the years? Why was that particular person chosen as a life-long friend?

4 Not all friendships remain healthy. What are the signs of an unhealthy friendship? How do you remove yourself from such a relationship?

5 Obviously, it's not possible to become friends with every person you meet. What is it that makes you move toward or away from a potential friend? The commitment of friendship?

6 Can friends be more important than family at times? How so?

7 Some people have one friend upon whom they can call, no matter what. What elements are present to create that kind of friendship?

8 In the end, the artichoke served as a metaphor for friendship. But in the beginning, it served as a barrier. What do you perceive as barriers to friendship?

9 What role does friendship play in marriage?

10 In the book, the author makes a point of saying that it takes time for a true friendship to develop. But time is one commodity of which women are in short supply. So how do you find the time?

Sights Unseen

Author:
Kaye Gibbons

Publisher: G.P. Putnam's Sons

First printing: 1995

Available in:
Hardcover, 256 pages. $19.95
(ISBN 0-399-13986-9)

Summary

Sights Unseen is the story of a family caught in the grip of a mother's erratic and frightening behavior. To her family, Maggie Barnes is the unpredictable wife, elusive mother, and adored daughter-in-law, and to her maid, Pearl, she is the mistress who must be cared for like a child in a difficult household. Young Hattie Barnes struggles to find a place in her mother's heart, and watches as Maggie is driven off to the hospital psychiatric ward. Only later will Hattie discover the deep-seated hopes and fears of the woman she loves unconditionally, and her inevitable connection to her family's past. Through Hattie's hushed voice, **Kaye Gibbons** tells the story of a troubled relationship and the courage it takes to see it through.

Recommended by *Time* magazine

"Some people might give up their second-born to write as well as Kaye Gibbons."

Author Biography

Kaye Gibbons is the author of *Charms for the Easy Life, A Cure for Dreams, A Virtuous Woman,* and *Ellen Foster.* She lives in Raleigh, North Carolina.

Topics to Consider

1 Hattie tries hard to understand her mother's motivation and thoughts when she is manic. Why is this so important to her? Do you think Hattie succeeds?

2 As a manic depressive, Maggie has violent mood swings. How does her family manage to survive between the mood swings?

3 Hattie and Freddy grow up practically in isolation – their father is wrapped up in their mother's madness and her illness prevents their friends from visiting. How does this isolation affect the children?

4 What is Pearl's role in the household? What effect does she have on Hattie? On Freddie?

5 After the incident with Freddie and Mr. Barnes at the beach, Hattie compares Maggie and Mr. Barnes' relationship to the attraction of two magnets: "Held one way, they rushed to collide, but if I turned one around the effect was the opposite" (page 154). Why are Maggie and Mr. Barnes so dependent on each other? What effect, if any, does this have on Maggie's illness?

6 When Mr. Barnes dies he bequeaths his home to Hattie upon the death of Miss Woodward. Why does he leave the house to her?

7 How does the non-linear structure of the novel add to your understanding of the narrator and her mother?

8 If her mother had never been sick, would Hattie's feelings toward her mother, which she discusses at the end of the novel, have been as strong?

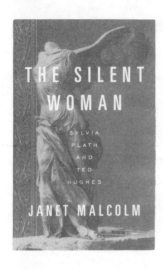

The Silent Woman
Sylvia Plath and Ted Hughes

Author:
Janet Malcolm

Publisher: Vintage

First printing: 1994

Available in:
Quality Paper, 224 pages. $12.00
(ISBN 0-679-75140-8)

Summary

In the years following her suicide in 1963, Sylvia Plath became the center of what was both a cult and an industry. Its principal product was an astonishing spate of biographies, each of which professed to tell the truth about the dead poet. But, as **Janet Malcolm** reminds us, "the biographer at work...is like the professional burglar." And the loot he or she brings back may not always be genuine. The author sifts through the competing claims and suspect motives of Plath's biographers and penetrates the reticence of her husband, Ted Hughes, who has by now become the ogre of the Plath legend. What emerges is a deft critique of the entire biographical genre and a book that comes closer to revealing the elusive Plath than any conventional biography ever could.

Recommended by Nell Bernstein, *San Francisco Examiner*

"Malcolm has expertly woven together threads of journalism, literary criticism, psychoanalysis, and biography itself to create a book that shows her a master of the craft..."

Author Biography

Janet Malcolm is the author of *Diana and Nikon, Psychoanalysis: The Impossible Profession, In the Freud Archives, The Journalist and the Murderer,* and *The Purloined Clinic.* She lives in New York City.

Topics to Consider

1 Who owns the facts of one's life? Does this situation change when one dies? Are the rights any different for the famous?

2 Why is it so difficult to get a handle on the real Sylvia Plath? Who knew her best? What makes her a more difficult subject than most?

3 How does biography differ from gossip? From propaganda? How can one evaluate the truth of a biography? Is it really nonfiction? What are the differences among biography, autobiography, and memoir?

4 Can one ever completely forfeit his or her right to privacy? Is there any way a famous person can forever protect his or her privacy or good name?

5 What challenges does a good biographer face? How does Malcolm define a good biographer? Does a biographer necessarily take sides among the involved parties?

6 Can a biographer make her character's story read like fiction? How does the story of Sylvia Plath, as told by Janet Malcolm, read?

7 How does the life of the biographer intersect with the life of his or her subject? What does Anne Stevenson's experience with *Bitter Fame* demonstrate?

8 What is the responsibility of a famous person's family in the telling of his or her life story? How do Aurelia Plath, Ted Hughes, and Olwyn Hughes behave in this regard? Is it a contest between the living and the dead? If so, who is likely to win?

9 Are any biographical sources pure? When using living sources, who can provide the best perspective? Does everyone have his or her own interest to advance? Can written sources from the subject herself, such as Plath's journal, be taken at face value?

The Substance of Things Hoped For

A Memoir of African-American Faith

Author:
Samuel DeWitt Proctor

Publisher: G.P. Putnam's Sons

First printing: January, 1996

Available in:
Hardcover, 288 pages. $21.95
(ISBN 0-399-14089-1)

Summary

In this compelling memoir, **Samuel DeWitt Proctor** invites us to share his lifetime of experiences and their lessons. He chronicles his family's journey — from his grandmother's slavery through the monumental victories of the NAACP, to his own involvement in the King Oasis — to show the common thread in the lives of millions of African-Americans: pure, enduring faith. This book passionately illustrates the author's tenet that lessons from the past can help create a more promising future. Dr. Proctor affirms that faith is powerful enough to respond to the despair of alienated young blacks locked in a cycle of denial and defeat today. Proctor believes faith can drive a national quest for a new kind of community — the first "genuine community" in which all African-Americans will participate fully and equally.

Recommended by Dr. Maya Angelou

"... Through the capable hands of Samuel Proctor, we have been given a book which is both prophecy and poetry."

Author Biography

Samuel DeWitt Proctor is Professor Emeritus at Rutgers University and Pastor Emeritus of the Abyssinian Baptist Church in Harlem. Having earned a doctorate in theology at Boston University, he served as associate director of the Peace Corps and as president of two colleges, among his many appointments. He lives in New Jersey.

Topics to Consider

1   "...the vast majority of slaves were denied any access to education as part of a well-documented conspiracy to forge a racial stereotype: namely, that blacks were less intelligent than whites and fundamentally unable to learn." (p. 3) Can you think of other "conspiracies" to the same end?

2   From early childhood, Proctor recalls teachers who spoke to children "in the subjunctive mood – not what is, but what *may be*...." Do you believe this same ideology to hold true in today's classrooms? Why or why not?

3   In the face of "white flight" to the suburbs, how can true integration be achieved and education standards be brought to an acceptable level in inner city schools today?

4   Dr. Proctor is repeatedly asked questions about his views of equal opportunity and affirmative action. How would your answers to the questions posed on pages 94-95 compare or differ with his?

5   The author believes that all parents should be held accountable for their children to the fullest extent of their ability. How does the need for both parents to work – sometimes more than one job – in order to provide for basic needs like food, clothing and shelter affect accountability?

6   Dr. Proctor states, "Believing that change is possible causes one to act in harmony with such faith." What are the greatest deterrents to believing that change is indeed possible?

7   "The most stubborn barrier to progress is the insistence that negative behavior stems from race, rather than from poverty and isolation." (p. 175) Do you agree? What can be done to break down this barrier?

8   Reflecting on the experience of Native Americans, the author asks "What choices might they have made that would have changed the outcome? What choices do they have now?" If these same questions are asked about other minority groups, how might the answers be similar? Different?

9   Even for the most impoverished, troubled youth, Dr. Proctor is adamant in his belief that "faith is the substance of things hoped for and the evidence of things not seen." What can be done to help young people discover such faith? What obstacles and forces must be overcome?

TREES
CALL for WHAT
THEY NEED

MELISSA KWASNY

Trees Call for What They Need

Author:
Melissa Kwasny

Publisher: Spinsters Ink

First printing: 1993

Available in:
Quality Paper, 200 pages. $9.95
(ISBN 0-933216-96-3)
Hardcover, 200 pages. $20.95
(ISBN 0-933216-97-1)

Summary

Trees Call for What They Need is the saga of three working-class women born at the turn of the century and their lives in the factory town of Pines, Indiana. *Trees* chronicles the evolution of the friendship between Nettie, a woolen mill worker and farmer; Aunt Till, a Spiritualist medium; and Marie, a Polish immigrant who owns the Poletown bar; and the impact upon their lives of the changes in the land around them. This is a novel about family and belonging, farming and caring for the land, the roots you put down and leave behind you. *Trees* is the story of three women's lives and how they made a difference without even trying.

Recommended by the *San Francisco Chronicle*

"It is the common human decency and vulnerability of Kwasny's characters, the quiet sense of strength and acceptance in the face of relentless and often incomprehensible change, that give Trees its distinctive but very believable appeal."

Author Biography

Melissa Kwasny was born in LaPorte, Indiana, and educated at the University of Montana. She is a poet and fiction writer. Her first novel, ***Modern Daughters and the Outlaw West,*** was published by Spinsters Ink in 1990. Ms. Kwasny lives in San Francisco and Montana.

Topics to Consider

1 How does Nettie's relationship with Art evolve? What makes their marriage last?

2 What survival techniques does Marie employ? What is the source of her strength?

3 Both Nettie and Marie lose a child — how does each woman deal with her loss?

4 How do the changes in the land affect each of the different principal characters?

5 At the end of Chapter 4, Nettie is unhappy at the prospect of farming the land. What causes her to change her attitude?

6 Ivy strikes the reader as remarkably independent and self-sufficient. Why does she marry Roy?

7 Reflect upon the four generations of women in Nettie's family: Ma, Nettie, Ivy, and Little Roy. How did these women differ from one another? Do they learn from one another? What do they learn?

8 Discuss the relationships between the principal characters in this novel.

9 Why do you think the author calls this novel "eco-feminist fiction?"

Until We Meet Again
A True Story of Love and Survival in the Holocaust

Authors:
Michael Korenblit
and Kathleen Janger

Publisher: Charles River Press

First printing: 1995

Available in:
Quality Paper, 336 pages. $13.95
(ISBN 0-9647124-0-7)

Summary

This horrifying yet inspirational story of two families decimated by the Holocaust begins in 1942 in a small town in Poland. When the Nazis arrive, 17-year-old Manya decides to leave her family and join her sweetheart, Meyer, in hiding with his family. Over the next three years, Manya and Meyer endure the loss of their parents and siblings, separation from each other, and the horror of concentration camps — sustained largely by their faith and love for each other and the help of courageous Polish Catholics.

Recommended by Michael Berenbaum, United States Holocaust Memorial Museum

"The Talmud says that creation began with one person in order to teach that whoever kills an individual destroys an entire world. Korenblit and Janger show that whoever retells the story of one person recovers an entire world, in all its complexity and drama...One can only admire this well-written work of filial devotion."

Author Biography

Michael Korenblit, son of Manya and Meyer, is an award-winning producer of educational documentaries now living in Oklahoma City. **Kathleen Janger,** a resident of McLean, Virginia, is a writer and educator.

Topics to Consider

1 The genesis of this book was **Michael Korenblit's** desire to learn about his parents' past. Which episode in the book do you think is his favorite to tell his children? Why? How does knowing their family history help people better understand themselves?

2 What do we learn in the book that helps explain Manya's decision to leave her family and join Meyer in hiding? What else might have motivated her decision?

3 Why is the diary Manya kept in the camps so important to her? Why is it so important to the guards that inmates not keep diaries?

4 Concentration camps were designed to "dehumanize" individuals. What does it mean to be "dehumanized"? In what ways do Manya and Meyer refuse to be dehumanized?

5 Discuss common images of Polish Catholics and Jews during the Holocaust, Nazi guards, little girls, and concentration camp inmates. Then, discuss how those stereotypes are undermined by individuals in the book.

6 In what ways do Manya and Meyer change during the course of the book? In what ways do they stay the same?

7 Discuss Manya's relationship with other women in the book. In what ways does she seem a conventional woman of the 1940s? In what ways does she seem unconventional?

8 What does it mean to be a "survivor"? Discuss differences and similarities between survivors of cancer, incest, or the Holocaust. How does being a survivor affect the rest of one's life?

9 Is it appropriate to judge Manya, Meyer, and others in the book according to usual moral standards? Why or why not?

10 What lessons can one draw from this book? Why is an understanding of the Holocaust important for Americans in the late 20th century?

Wonder Boys

Author:
Michael Chabon

Publisher: Picador USA

First printing: 1995

Available in:
Quality Paper, 384 pages. $13.00
(ISBN 0-312-14094-0)

Summary

Grady Tripp is a former prodigy, a pot-smoking, philandering middle-aged novelist who has stalled on a 2,611-page unfinished opus titled *Wonder Boys*. Grady's student James Leer is a troubled young writer obsessed by Hollywood suicides, prone to petty thievery, and at work on his own first manuscript. Joined by Grady's sexually ambitious editor Terry Crabtree, the trio careens on a wild nighttime odyssey through the streets, bars, and environs of Pittsburgh, in search of past promise, future fame, and an ever-elusive vision of redemption through art and language.

Recommended by Shelby Hearon, *Chicago Tribune*

"[A] wise, wildly funny story ... Chabon is a flat-out wonderful writer — evocative and inventive, pointed and poignant."

Author Biography

Michael Chabon's first novel, *The Mysteries of Pittsburgh*, was a national bestseller. His short stories have been published in *The New Yorker* and *Esquire*, and were collected in a volume, *A Model World*. He lives in Los Angeles with his wife and daughter.

Topics to Consider

1 The narrator, Grady Tripp, describes Albert Vetch as "the first real writer" he ever knew, an example he had "been living up to ever since." What was his example? In this novel's terms, what makes a "real writer"? Who else qualifies?

2 What is the "midnight disease"? Is it an affliction only of writers?

3 What is the relationship between the authors and their fictional works? Do they see their works as others see them?

4 The characters in this book write fiction. Are their lives based on truth?

5 James Leer is obsessed with Hollywood. How are romance and shadows juxtaposed in the movies and in this book?

6 Through the course of the book, Grady Tripp fills his trunk with a dead dog, a dead snake, and a tuba. What is the significance of his acquisition of these items? His relinquishment of them? Do the items themselves symbolize anything?

7 Much of the main characters' behavior seems self-indulgent and drug-induced. How do their escapades relate to the statement that "all male friendships are essentially quixotic: they last only so long as each man is willing to polish the shaving-bowl helmet, climb on his donkey, and ride off after the other in pursuit of illusive glory and questionable adventure"?

8 The cover of the book features several quotes from reviews citing its humor. Give examples of scenes you found humorous. What elements are necessary to perceive a situation as humorous?

9 How would you describe the characters' sense of family or of family responsibility?

10 Grady Tripp muses about his destiny — where he might live, whom he might love, work he might do. Does he realize any of his dreams? Is he satisfied with his life? What role has destiny played, if any, in your life?

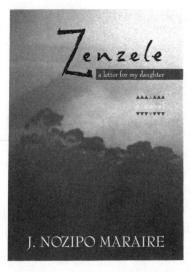

Zenzele

A Letter for My Daughter

Author:
J. Nozipo Maraire

Publisher: Crown

First printing: 1995

Available in:
Hardcover, 208 pages, $20.00
(ISBN 0-517-70242-8)

Summary

In this novel – written as a letter from a Zimbabwean mother to her daughter, a student at Harvard – the author transforms the lessons of life into a lyrical narrative about love, war, separation, and the very meaning of being a woman. Weaving history and memories, disappointments and dreams, this letter is a gift from one generation to the next. With humor and poignancy, the mother writes of the clash between old and new, between the "European" way and the traditional ways of the African people ... *"I hope that you will pardon this curious distillation of traditional African teaching, social commentary, and maternal concern ... it is an old woman's privilege to impart her wisdom."* Zenzele is at once the intimate story of a mother and her hopes for her daughter and a compelling depiction of the birth of a new Africa.

Recommended by Rita Mae Brown

"In this letter written by a mother to her daughter, we each become her child, enriched by her knowledge born of laughter as well as pain."

Author Biography

J. Nozipo Maraire, a native of Zimbabwe, graduated from Harvard and received a medical degree at Columbia. A writer, a neurosurgeon, and an art gallery owner, she lives in New Haven, Connecticut. *Zenzele* is her first novel.

Topics to Consider

1 This is a letter from an African mother to her daughter. What are the characteristics of it that are particular to their circumstances? What about it is more universal?

2 The mother speaks of being "bewildered by the task of motherhood, that precarious balance between total surrender and totalitarianism." Where do you think she positions herself on that continuum? What visions do she and her daughter share and where do they diverge?

3 What does the village of Chakowa represent?

4 Many of the stories relate the way of life in the time of the mother's youth. Is there anything more than generational change at work here? Could similar advice be given to any young person going out on his or her own?

5 When looking at the University catalogue Zenzele exclaims, "There is no limit." Does her mother see limits for her? What does the mother see as her role in her daughter's life?

6 As the mother sifts through her memories to share with her daughter, what does she reveal about herself? Does she harbor any regrets? Of what is she most proud?

7 Contrast the story of Mukoma Byron with that of "Sister Africa". How do they differ in their relationship to their families and to Africa? Are there any similarities between them?

8 What has the mother learned about prejudice? What is the nature of the western challenge to African culture, the post-colonial syndrome?

9 The mother's letter covers many subjects and ideas. What does she hope Zenzele will learn about love? Wisdom? Fate or destiny? God?

10 Although this book is written as fiction, what would you infer about the author, who is an American-educated native of Zimbabwe now living in the United States?

Resources

Newsletters

Reverberations NewsJournal, the publication of the Association of Book Group Readers and Leaders. Annual membership including subscription is $30. Contact: ABGRL, Box 885, Highland Park, IL 60035

BOOKNEWS AND VIEWS, quarterly newsletter of Books, Etcetera. Annual subscription is $10. Contact: Books, Etcetera, 228 Commercial Street #1957, Nevada City, CA 95959, (916) 478-9400.

Literary Trips

Literary Getaways to Northern California with Judith Palarz. Book discussions and sightseeing for lovers of literature. Two days, two nights at a Bed & Breakfast Inn in Nevada City, the Napa Valley or Half Moon Bay. Contact: Books, Etcetera, 228 Commercial Street #1957, Nevada City, CA 95959, (916) 478-9400.

Books

Minnesota Women's Press Great Books. Contact: Minnesota Women's Press, 771 Raymond Avenue, Saint Paul, MN 55114, (612) 646-3968.

The Reading Group Handbook by Rachel W. Jacobsohn. Published by Hyperion, ISBN 0-7868-8002-3, $10.95

The New York Public Library Guide to Reading Groups by Rollene Saal. Published by Crown, ISBN 0-517-88357-0, $11.

What to Read: The Essential Guide for Reading Group Members and Other Book Lovers by Mickey Pearlman. Published by Harper Perennial, ISBN 0-06-095061-7, $9.

The Book Group Book: A Thoughtful Guide to Forming and Enjoying a Stimulating Book Discussion Group by Ellen Slezak. Published by Chicago Review Press, ISBN 1-55652-195-2, $9.95

Index by Author

Index by Author

(continued)

Index by Author

Index by Genre

Non-fiction

Index by Genre

Non-fiction (continued)

Fiction

Index by Genre

Fiction (continued)

Index by Subject

1996

January
S	M	T	W	T	F	S
	1	2	3	4	5	6
7	8	9	10	11	12	13
14	15	16	17	18	19	20
21	22	23	24	25	26	27
28	29	30	31			

February
S	M	T	W	T	F	S
				1	2	3
4	5	6	7	8	9	10
11	12	13	14	15	16	17
18	19	20	21	22	23	24
25	26	27	28	29		

March
S	M	T	W	T	F	S
					1	2
3	4	5	6	7	8	9
10	11	12	13	14	15	16
17	18	19	20	21	22	23
24	25	26	27	28	29	30
31						

April
S	M	T	W	T	F	S
	1	2	3	4	5	6
7	8	9	10	11	12	13
14	15	16	17	18	19	20
21	22	23	24	25	26	27
28	29	30				

May
S	M	T	W	T	F	S
			1	2	3	4
5	6	7	8	9	10	11
12	13	14	15	16	17	18
19	20	21	22	23	24	25
26	27	28	29	30	31	

June
S	M	T	W	T	F	S
						1
2	3	4	5	6	7	8
9	10	11	12	13	14	15
16	17	18	19	20	21	22
23	24	25	26	27	28	29
30						

July
S	M	T	W	T	F	S
	1	2	3	4	5	6
7	8	9	10	11	12	13
14	15	16	17	18	19	20
21	22	23	24	25	26	27
28	29	30	31			

August
S	M	T	W	T	F	S
				1	2	3
4	5	6	7	8	9	10
11	12	13	14	15	16	17
18	19	20	21	22	23	24
25	26	27	28	29	30	31

September
S	M	T	W	T	F	S
1	2	3	4	5	6	7
8	9	10	11	12	13	14
15	16	17	18	19	20	21
22	23	24	25	26	27	28
29	30					

October
S	M	T	W	T	F	S
		1	2	3	4	5
6	7	8	9	10	11	12
13	14	15	16	17	18	19
20	21	22	23	24	25	26
27	28	29	30	31		

November
S	M	T	W	T	F	S
					1	2
3	4	5	6	7	8	9
10	11	12	13	14	15	16
17	18	19	20	21	22	23
24	25	26	27	28	29	30

December
S	M	T	W	T	F	S
1	2	3	4	5	6	7
8	9	10	11	12	13	14
15	16	17	18	19	20	21
22	23	24	25	26	27	28
29	30	31				

NOTES

Paz & Associates

This publication was developed and produced by Paz & Associates, whose mission is to join with publishers and bookstores to develop resources and skills that promote books and reading. We offer workshops, individual consulting and printed resources including the monthly newsletter *Independent Bookselling Today!*, *The Training Guide to FrontLine Bookselling* and the training video *Exceptional FrontLine Bookselling: It's All About Service.* Look for our site on the World Wide Web at *Pazbookbiz.com.*

For additional copies of this publication, please call your local bookstore or contact us at the address and phone number below. We will be happy to let you know of a bookstore in your area that has obtained copies of *Reading Group Choices.* Quantities are limited.

Paz & Associates
2106 Twentieth Avenue South
Nashville, TN 37212-4312

(800) 260-8605
(615) 298-2303

Women's National Book Association

WNBA is an organization that brings together women and men who value the written word. There are ten chapters located in Atlanta, Binghamton, Boston, Dallas, Detroit, Los Angeles, Nashville, New York, San Francisco, and Washington D.C. To find out how to contact a chapter near you, or to learn how to start a new chapter, write or call:

WNBA
160 Fifth Avenue
New York, NY 10010

(212) 675-7805